EVERYTHING®

C·R·A·F·T·S

CREATE YOUR OWN

GREETING CARDS

**Step-by-Step Instructions
for Creating
Unique Cards for Any Occasion**

Edited by Courtney Nolan

Adams Media
Avon, Massachusetts

An Everything® Series Book.
Everything® and everything.com® are registered trademarks of F+W Publications, Inc.

Published by Adams Media, an F+W Publications Company
57 Littlefield Street, Avon, MA 02322 U.S.A.
www.adamsmedia.com

ISBN: 1-59337-226-4
Printed in the United States of America.

J I H G F E D C B A

Library of Congress Cataloging-in-Publication Data
Everything crafts--create your own greeting cards / edited by Courtney Nolan.
       p.   cm.
(Everything series book)
ISBN 1-59337-226-4
1. Greeting cards. I. Title: Create your own greeting cards. II. Nolan, Courtney.
III. Title. IV. Series: Everything series.

TT872.E335 2004
745.594'1--dc22

                         2004009935

This publication is designed to provide accurate and authoritative information with regard to the subject matter covered. It is sold with the understanding that the publisher is not engaged in rendering legal, accounting, or other professional advice. If legal advice or other expert assistance is required, the services of a competent professional person should be sought.

—From a *Declaration of Principles* jointly adopted by a Committee of the American Bar Association and a Committee of Publishers and Associations

Many of the designations used by manufacturers and sellers to distinguish their products are claimed as trademarks. Where those designations appear in this book and Adams Media was aware of a trademark claim, the designations have been printed with initial capital letters.

This book is available at quantity discounts for bulk purchases.
For information, call 1-800-872-5627.

Some material in this publication has been adapted and compiled from the following previously published works:

McGraw, MaryJo   *Greeting Card Magic with Rubber Stamps* ©2000 (F+W Publications, Inc.)
McGraw, MaryJo   *Making Greeting Cards with Creative Materials* ©2001 (F+W Publications, Inc.)
                  Greeting Cards Made Easy ©2000 (David & Charles/F+W Publications, Inc.)
                  Decorative Papers Made Easy ©2000 (David & Charles/F+W Publications, Inc.)

Photography by: John Gollop and Christine Polomsky. Illustrations by: Fred Fieber at Red Crayola

Part Three • 69

Get Crafty: Cards for Any Occasion

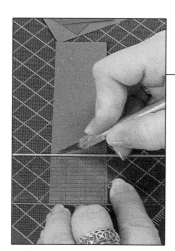

Part Four • 109

Get Inspired: Cards for Love

Part Five • 125

Get Festive: Cards for Holidays

Welcome to the *Everything® Crafts* Series!

If you want to get in touch with your inner creativity but aren't sure where to begin, you've already completed Step One—choosing the perfect resource to help you get started. The EVERYTHING® CRAFTS books are ideal for beginners because they provide illustrated, step-by-step instruction for creating fun—and unique—projects.

The EVERYTHING® CRAFTS books bring the craft world back to the basics, providing easy-to-follow direction on finding appropriate tools and materials to learn new craft techniques. These clear and readable books guide you every step of the way, from beginning until end, teaching you tips and tricks to get your craft to look just right.

So sit back and enjoy. This experience is all about introducing you to the world of crafts—and, most of all, learning EVERYTHING you can!

A note to our readers:

The card projects you find in *EVERYTHING® CRAFTS—Create Your Own Greeting Cards* are precious to those who created them. Each crafter has discovered just the right mix of colors, products, and materials to produce the cards you will find in this book. With that, we would like to offer many thanks to the individuals who have offered much of their time and effort into either contributing projects or supplying materials for the card designs in this book.

First, a special thanks goes to: MaryJo McGraw; everyone at North Light Books, including Jane Friedman, Tricia Waddell, Christine Polomsky, Sally Finnegan, and Greg Albert; everyone at David & Charles; Jill Millis, Cheryl Owen, Jan Cox, and John Underwood.

Of course, a special thanks goes to craft store and company owners for supplying each and every crafter with the necessary tools and materials so that readers like you can create and enjoy the projects in this book.

—The Editors, EVERYTHING® CRAFTS *Series*

Introduction

Everything® Crafts—Create Your Own Greeting Cards is packed full of fun and unique projects that will have your friends begging for your secrets. Everyone knows handmade greeting cards—or at least cards that *look* handmade—are available in stores everywhere. Even department stores are selling fancy cards with sassy adornments and funky paper. If you're tired of actually *paying* for a card that you can make, you've come to the right place.

This is a book for you, the beginner. *Everything® Crafts—Create Your Own Greeting Cards* gives you step-by-step instruction on *exactly* how to create the cards you'll find inside. From unique notes for friends and loved ones to festive greetings for the holidays, you'll blow your friends away with your creativity.

Feel free to get crazy—mix and match with your own stamps, photos, and embellishments. Looking to score a few points? Turn to the projects labeled "Extra Credit." These involve a little more work and creativity but the end result is surely worth it. Not sure how you're going to send out your masterpiece? No problem! Simply design the matching envelope, or create a gift tag and deliver the card personally.

Everything® Crafts—Create Your Own Greeting Cards breaks down each step so that you don't feel overwhelmed or lost. The visuals are carefully coordinated with the instructions to make it impossible for you to miss a step or make a mistake. Look for important tips and hints to keep you in the loop about the way certain supplies can react or misbehave, and read up on expert advice for making the card craft process easier. Use the inserts to see your favorite card in color.

So go play! All the techniques and instructions in this book are simple and easily mastered with minimal practice. Get out all of your supplies and set no limits! Be creative and be daring!

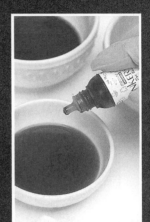

Part One

Card Basics:

Everything You Should Know about Tools, Materials, and Techniques

Tools and Materials

Below are tools and materials you will need to create the greeting card projects in this book. In some cases, inexpensive alternatives are listed if available, and suggestions are made about whether it is absolutely necessary for you to purchase a particular tool. To learn more about store locations and Web site information, please see the resources listed on page 146.

The Essentials

Equipment necessary for creating cards:

- Card or thick paper
- Sharp scissors
- Double-sided tape
- Ruler
- Pencil
- Tacky glue
- Craft knife and cutting mat
- White paper
- Glue gun

Rubber Stamps

There are usually three parts to a rubber stamp: the mount, the cushion, and the die. Quality mounts are made from hardwood and the cushion is made of foam. The die is the most important part of the stamp because it transfers the design, and should be closely trimmed.

Paper and Stamping

Most of the projects in this book require high-grade papers and cardstock. Don't skimp on the paper—it will show in your final product. One of the papers you should have is a **translucent vellum**. Be sure you can see through it, as there are many types of vellum that are opaque.

Vellum

Vellum is really translucent vellum, or a sheer paper that can be found in all stamp, paper, and scrapbooking stores. Perfect for paper overlay work, many types come with designs already printed on one side. Its color can be altered with dye ink.

Paper

The thicker the paper or cardstock (card), the more adhesive you need to adhere it. Most heavy porous papers may need extra time for a glue or adhesive to sink in and set. The more textured the paper, the more you must work glue or adhesive onto the surface.

Materials for Cards ▌ Almost any material can be used to create a greeting card, but the important things to keep in mind when making your selections are:

- The way the card will be folded
- Whether there will be a window opening
- The weight and size of the surface decoration

Each of the above will affect the balance and stability of the card, and should be considered when choosing material.

Chipboard

Chipboard is an inexpensive, useful material, which is the same material used to make cereal boxes and the backs of paper tablets. You can substitute mat board or any recycled cardboard for chipboard.

Inks

There are three basic ink types: dye, pigment, and solvent.

Dye-based pads are the type you see lying around the house or office. Dye-based ink is water-soluble.

Pigment inks are now widely available through stamp and gift stores and are a good choice when using uncoated papers. They are also used for embossing and for archival applications, like scrapbooking.

Solvent-based inks are used mainly for stamping on unusual surfaces like wood, plastic, and ceramic. Use them for a nice, crisp, black outline that won't smear like dye inks do.

Acrylic Inks

These inks can be found near calligraphy or airbrush supplies in craft stores. Acrylics are very thin, which makes them perfect for washes and drip applications. Most acrylic inks can be mixed together with Diamond Glaze, gesso, and many kinds of paint.

Dye Re-Inkers

Dye re-inkers are the small bottles of ink you normally use to refill your dye-based inkpads. For rubberstamping projects, use re-inkers to color **Diamond Glaze**—by adding a few drops, you can make a paint that is transparent when dry. Be careful when using inks straight from the bottle—they are highly concentrated and will easily stain clothing. Remember to use the smallest amount of ink possible because you can always add more.

Embossing powders

Embossing powders are required for many of the rubber stamp card projects.

To use embossing powder:

- Stamp an image with pigment or embossing ink.
- Sprinkle the powder over the wet ink and shake off the excess.
- Use a heat gun to melt the powder and create a raised design.

Try to have a variety of colors in supply since embossing looks great in just about every color. Just so you know, embossing powder comes in solid-color and multi-color forms.

Double-Sided Tape

Double-sided tape comes in many varieties. The double-sided tape used in this book includes **mosaic tape**, a paper-lined tape that is thin, embossable, heat resistant, and great for layering; **cellophane double-sided tape**, which is great for layering, especially with transparent papers; and **double-sided foam tape**, which is perfect when you need to add height to cards.

Acetate

The acetate used for the rubber stamp projects in this book can be found in stamp stores almost everywhere. Be sure you purchase **embossable acetate** (also known as "window plastic") in case you want to heat the piece. The same is true of heavy cold laminate—it should be embossable. The thicker the laminate is, the better for the rubber stamp projects because of the strong handling the pieces need to endure.

Cold Laminate

There are some laminates that need heat to make them adhere. Cold laminate, however, is an extremely clear, heavy acetate that is sticky on one side. This makes it an easier laminate to use and no other equipment is necessary to make it work. Cold laminate will give any paper surface a high-gloss look and can be embossed.

Decoration Ideas ▮ Here are some great ways to spruce up and embellish your cards:

- Foam sheet or cork
- Metal sheeting or metal cut from pet food tins
- Fabric, ribbon, lace, or Hessian
- Jewels, mirrors, and old jewelry
- Shells, stones, or beads
- Buttons or mosaic tiles
- Dried flowers, bark, twigs, leaves, or raffia
- Pompoms, chenille sticks, or toy eyes
- Psychedelic paper or handmade paper
- Cake decorating, silk, or paper flowers
- Outliner paste or glass paint
- Metallic pens, glitter glue, or watercolor pencils

Gesso

Gesso is a primer paint that can be used in all sorts of projects as a mixing agent. Use gesso as a primer for **canvas** and **Styrofoam**. It comes in black and white and can be found at art supply stores.

Accessories

Accessories like **thread**, **beads**, **paper cord**, **tassels**, and **gift tags** can be found at most stamp stores, and you can also find them at specialty stores for beads and needlecrafts. Try checking out your local office supply store—this is a great outlet for finding unusual items to use as decorations for your greeting cards.

Metal Accessories

Some projects include metals like copper wire, thin copper sheets, or fun metal shapes as embellishments. These items should not be difficult to locate at your local craft, stamp, and hardware stores.

Picture Pebbles

Picture pebbles or glass marbles, have one flat surface. These come in a wide variety of sizes and colors and are available in many stamp or craft stores. When the pebble is placed over an image, it mag-nifies the design, which is perfect when using tiny photos. If you decide to use colored pebbles, choose light hues. Clear ones are perfect for darker pieces. In general, pebbles are great for quick jewelry projects.

Watch Crystals

Watch crystals can really spruce up your crafts in a plethora of ways. You can find these at paper and stamp stores. Crystals can be filled with beads, seeds, sand, small toys, or pictures. The watch crystals used in this book are inexpensive and plastic. For other watch parts or more expensive crystals such as glass, check out the Resources list on page 146 or do an online search for auction sites.

Beads

The glass beads usually used in rubberstamping projects are tiny, holeless, and coated with a metallic finish. Feel free to experiment with other types of beads, remembering that the smaller the better so that they stay attached to the card and make it safely through the mail.

Mica Tiles

These tiles are compressed slices of mica that can be cut and layered. They are a decoration as well as a protective covering for photos. Mica tiles are heat-resistant, acid-free, and lightweight.

Bone Folder

The bone folder is a great tool for scoring paper and smoothing down creases. Some are made from bone, while others are made from resin or wood. They come in several lengths and are very helpful in many crafts.

Eyelets

Similar to grommets, using the setting tool will roll down the back of the eyelet. This tool and colored ones are available through stamp and paper stores.

Brayers

Brayers come in so many varieties it is sometimes difficult to decide which one to buy. The best value for a great brayer is a detachable 4" soft rubber one. It will handle most jobs and is easier to clean. You will also find sponge, acrylic, hard rubber, and wood brayers—each type yields a different result.

Craft Knives

A craft knife is an invaluable tool when creating greeting cards or other stamp projects. The blade should be pointed and very sharp, so be sure to change it often to ensure clean cuts.

Punches and Cutters

A number of projects use a variety of paper punches, including circle, square, spiral, and leaf ones. Think about investing in a circle cutter, which can be adjusted to cut circles in a range of diameters—they are usually found at most craft stores. If you don't have a hole punch, sometimes an **awl** will work just as well.

Heat Gun

Look for a heat gun that is especially made for stamping, as they are usually geared at a safe temperature for craft projects. Remember to keep your heat gun away from your cutting mat as it can distort the surface and create difficulties when you go to use it.

Fabric Bond

Fabric bond is an excellent way to adhere fibrous materials together, especially handmade papers.

Remember to:

- Accurately measure and cut the rectangle of paper to be used for the card, making sure all corners are exactly 90-degree angles.
- Work the back or blunt side of a craft knife to score the fold lines.
- Use a ballpoint pen to draw design lines onto foam sheets, and always cut using a craft knife and cutting mat.
- Cut metal sheeting with scissors.
- Punch holes in metal sheeting using a punching tool, on a soft wooden board with a rubber mallet.
- Emboss patterns onto the back of metal sheeting using a blunt pencil or an empty ballpoint pen.
- Use a ruler to draw lines with a paint pen, and turn it onto its convex side as this will stop the ink from spreading.
- Wet edges of handmade paper before tearing.
- Use deckle-edged scissors to give card edges a decorative look.
- Hang a mobile behind a window opening using invisible embroidery thread.

Shrink Plastic

Most shrink plastics shrink by 40 to 50 percent. You can shrink the plastic using a heat gun on a heat-safe surface (not your cutting mat), but be aware that the piece will might not heat evenly. Be careful so that you don't get burned and keep shrinking the plastic until you get it down to a size you want.

Tassels and Cords

Tassels make a great addition to cards and the ones used in projects in this book are available at most stamp or craft stores. As you will see on the pages that follow, paper cord is an extremely versatile decorative item also found at craft stores. Both tassels and cords are usually sold in a wide assortment of colors.

Templates

Plastic and brass templates are a great investment. They last forever, are inexpensive, and there are many varieties available. Look for envelope, box, and card templates at your local craft store.

Pastels and Water-Soluble Crayons

Pastels and water-soluble crayons are available in stamp and art supply stores everywhere. Crayons that are soy-based are usually a better buy since they have a creamy texture and are loaded with pigment.

Powdered Pigments

Powdered pigments are raw pigments used for a variety of purposes, including making homemade paints. You can also use these pigments as a surface coating on paper or collage projects. Powdered pigments do need what is known as a **binder** to keep them adhered to your project. In this book, **Diamond Glaze** will be used as a binder. Other options include **white glue**, **paint mediums**, **gum arabic**, or **spray fixative**. Mixing any of these with the powdered pigments will create a colored medium you can apply to surfaces as needed. **PearlEx** powdered pigments are used actively in many of the projects in this book.

Paint Pens

There are types of paint pens where you can apply the paint with a brush in pen form and they will work effectively only on paper. For all nonporous surfaces like clays, plastics, wood, chipboard, and metal, you will need a permanent kind of paint pen. **Krylon Gold** and **Silver and Copper Leafing pens** keep their true metallic colors on most surfaces.

Techniques

Apply Specific Skills to Your Card Creations

There are several techniques that you can use during the card-making process. You'll find that each of the following techniques has at least one corresponding project that requires you to use the instructions from the technique to create the card. These easy instructions are for you to experiment with and to learn more about so that you can put the cards together.

These lessons will be a foundation for you to build on what you learn by mixing and matching your skills from one creation to another. Don't fret if you make a mistake with any of the projects at first—this is part of the learning process. Making a mistake will only strengthen your abilities and add to the craft experience—just relax and be creative—your imagination is in charge!

Basic Envelope Templates

Envelope templates are perfect for tiny messages. Great for exquisite embellishments like gold, silk, or velvet, as well as small charms or tags, these little packages are dressy enough to enclose money or a gift certificate.

 Get Started:

vellum • pencil • bone folder • scissors • paintbrush • white glue • envelope glue

1 Start by tracing the template on page 11 lightly onto the vellum with a pencil.

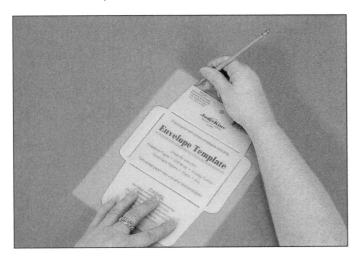

Switch It Up

A vellum that is tinted and transparent was used for this project, but know that there are many colors available. Some are even embedded with glitter or confetti.

2 Using a bone folder or a stylus, score the vellum using the slots in the template.

3 Cut out the envelope, using the pencil lines as a guide. Remove any pencil marks with a soft eraser.

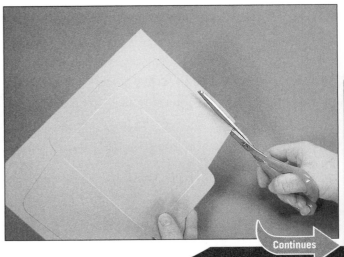

Continues

Switch It Up

Use recycled old magazines, outdated calendar pages, and any gift-wrap paper for new envelopes. For a more personal envelope, copy your family photos on a color copier!

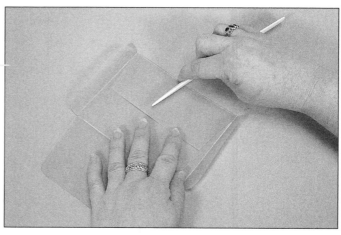

4 Fold along the score marks. Burnish the creases with the side of the bone folder.

5 Using a paintbrush and a small amount of clear-drying glue, cover the lower half of the envelope seams. Fold and seal the seams. Do not use this glue for the envelope flap.

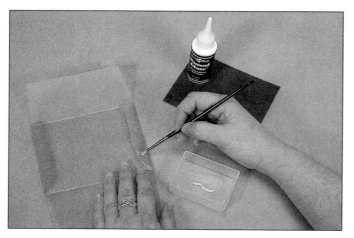

6 Using the recipe to the right, make a batch of "lickable" envelope glue. Apply the glue to the top flap of the envelope.

◆ *Most projects are specific about explaining how to make an envelope to match or fit the card you will create. This particular template is directly related to the Mini Message card craft on page 32.*

Envelope-Flap Glue Recipe

This glue will keep for a few weeks in a cool place.

18 tbs. white vinegar

1 small package gelatin, any flavor

1 Bring the vinegar to a boil. Add the gelatin and stir until completely dissolved.

2 Pour mixture into a small container with a tight seal and allow to cool completely for at least one hour.

3 Brush the cooled glue onto the envelope flap. Allow to dry. Now you may store the envelopes. To use, moisten the flap and seal.

Cut line _____

Fold line _ _ _

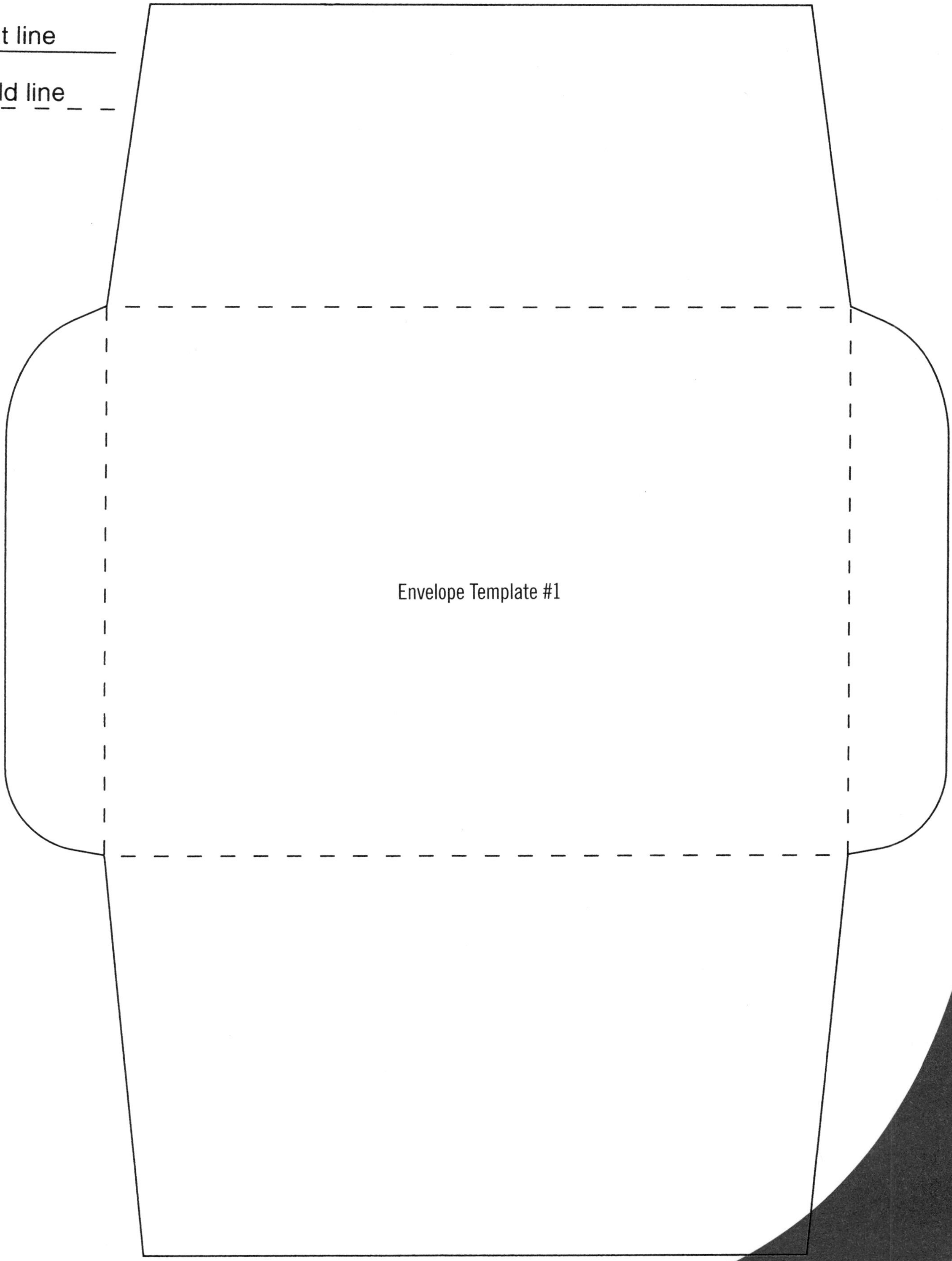

Envelope Template #1

Use this as a guide when creating an envelope for your homemade card.

- Draw a rectangle on a thick piece of paper—it should be slightly larger than your card
- Fold side flaps in and the bottom flaps up
- Add flaps to the four edges
- Score along dotted lines
- Glue together

Envelope Template #2

Creating a Mold and Deckle

Use this tool for papermaking and to assist you in creating other fine card projects in this book.

 Get Started:

8 pieces of wood: four pieces ¾ × ⅜ inches long, and four pieces 8 inches long • PVA glue • 4 rust-proof nails • fine net • water • steel staples • waterproof PVA glue

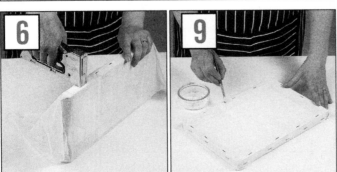

1 Arrange two of the longer pieces of wood, and the two shorter pieces together to form a rectangle. This is the mold.

2 Use PVA glue to hold the pieces together. Leave mold untouched so glue can dry, about 2 hours or as per the glue manufacturer's instructions.

3 When the glue has completely dried, hammer two rust-proof nails into each corner of the mold, making sure the nails are long enough to go through both lengths of wood.

4 Repeat Step 3 for deckle.

5 Cut a piece of fine net to fit over the mold.

6 Wet the net and attach it to the frame using steel staples.

7 Start stapling the middle of each side, pulling tightly as you work. Keep the net taut as you staple around the frame. When the net dries it will become tighter.

8 Cut any excess net.

9 Seal the edges with waterproof PVA glue. The mold and deckle should be the same size when held together.

◆ *The mold and deckle is used in the papermaking principles technique.*

Papermaking Principles

Go crazy with the papermaking process! You're now not only creating your own greeting cards, you're also creating the very paper you're using to make some of these projects! Go wild!

 Get Started:

paper for pulp (computer paper, paper bags, and envelopes) • bucket • water • mold and deckle (directions on how to make one on page 13) • handheld liquidizer or piece of wood • plastic tray (to use as a vat) • paper napkins (optional) • newspaper • hardboard • wet kitchen cloths • 2 clean bricks or heavy weights • rolling pin (optional)

Pulp

1 Look at the paper that you will use for pulp. Discard any sheets covered in glue and remove any staples.

2 Tear the paper for pulp into small squares, about the size of postage stamps.

3 Place torn paper into a bucket and fill with cold water to cover. Leave the bucket to soak for several days. The water level will decrease as it soaks into the paper.

This is normal. When you notice water loss, add water to the bucket, making sure torn paper is always covered.

4 In the meantime, create your mold and deckle (page 13).

5 After the paper has finished soaking, empty any remaining water that is in the bucket.

Tearing paper

Placing torn paper in bucket with water

Beating paper into pulp

6 Using a handheld liquidizer or a piece of wood, beat the paper to a mushy pulp. Mash until smooth and creamy (this will take some time).

7 Fill a plastic tray halfway with water. Pour pulp into the tray so that there is a ratio of approximately $1/3$ pulp to $2/3$ water. Stir the pulp and water together.

To Add Color to Your Paper

Tear paper napkins (in a color of your choice) into small squares and add them to the pulp after Step 7; stir well.

Filling plastic tray

Adding color to paper

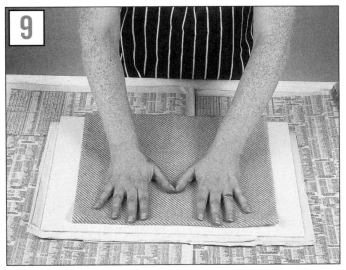

Preparing the workspace

8 Cover your work surface with paper because the pulp will be very moist to handle.

9 Place a folded newspaper in the center of your space. On top of this, place a piece of hardboard and a wet cloth. **Note:** Be careful to keep the cloth smooth to keep from marking up the finished paper.

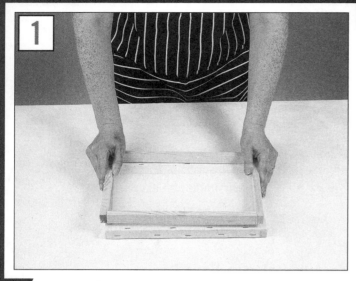
Placing the deckle on top of mold

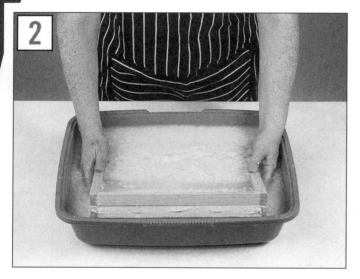
Sliding mold and deckle into mixture

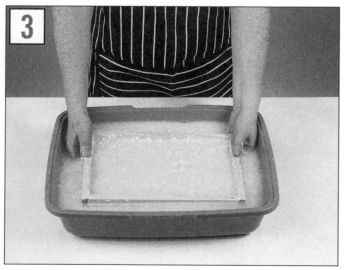
Finding a good balance of pulp

Paper

1 Give the pulp another good stir. Place the deckle on top of the mold, with the net side facing up. Line up the edges exactly. Press the pieces firmly together.

2 Slide the mold and deckle into the mixture slowly, at an angle, working from the far side of the vat. Note: If you have trouble collecting pulp on the net part of the mold and deckle, the ratio of pulp to water may be incorrect. Adjust the ratio so as to avoid too much pulp or else the paper will be thick and lumpy; if too little pulp, paper will be thin and holey.

3 Straighten the mold and deckle so that the net is just below the surface of pulp. Gently lift mold and deckle to check that you have an even amount of thickness of pulp on the net. Should you be unhappy with the thickness of pulp, scrape it back into vat and begin again.

Tips for Making Paper

- Use a plastic sheet and plenty of newspaper to protect your work surface.
- Clean the mold and deckle thoroughly between making each sheet of paper.
- Use a cat litter tray as a vat for making paper and for marbling.
- Let as much water drain away as possible before you transfer the newly made sheet of paper to the kitchen cloth.
- Adjust the ratio of pulp to water in the vat between making each sheet so that you have $1/3$ pulp to $2/3$ water.

4 Lift mold and deckle out of pulp, gently rocking it back and forth and from side to side. Note: This helps fibers settle to result in a flatter sheet of paper. Be careful: do not overdo rocking or pulp will become holey.

5 Allow any excess water to drain; this can take several minutes. If you want, place the mold and deckle across one corner of the vat to drain as you wait.

6 Take deckle from top of mold. If water is caught in inside edges of deckle, allow it to drain, keeping the mold flat until the water is gone. Turn mold over so that the new sheet of paper faces down.

7 Transfer the paper to the work surface quickly. Should the paper fall from the mold, scrape it back into the vat and begin making the sheet again.

8 In one gentle movement, place the mold on to the cloth, press down on one of the shorter edges, and lift up on the opposite edge.

9 Roll mold up and away, leaving the sheet of paper on the cloth. It might take a few tries for you to get an even layer of paper on the net, and to get the sheet to stay put on the work surface. If anything goes wrong, simply start again.

Allowing excess water to drain

Placing and pressing mold on cloth

Taking deckle from top of mold

Rolling mold up and away

Continues

Covering the final sheet

Placing the bricks or weights

10 Place a damp cloth on top of the new sheet of paper.

11 Smooth cloth to remove any wrinkles, making sure the surface is perfectly flat.

12 Make four or five more sheets and place them on top of the first with damp cloths separating each sheet. Cover the final sheet with a damp cloth then cover the stack with a clean piece of hardboard.

13 Place two clean bricks on top of the hardboard and allow several hours for excess water to soak up in the cloth or run out on the paper.

Tips for Making Texture Paper

Use these techniques to create paper with a textured surface:

- Leave the paper to dry on textured fabric like tweed, a lace mat, or patterned net curtain.
- Push objects into the damp paper to make a raised pattern.
- Add dried lentils and split peas to the damp paper.
- Add ribbon roses, beads, metal foil, and scraps of paper to the surface of the pulp.
- Drop pressed flowers and leaves, seeds, and potpourri into the pulp.

Couching

It has nothing to do with your sofa. It's actually the part of the papermaking process where you stack, press, and dry the newly made paper.

14 Place a piece of plastic on your work surface. Remove the hardboard and cloth from the top of the stack.

15 Carefully work to take off a cloth and its sheet of paper, and lay it on the plastic sheet to dry. Note: The paper will be quite strong at this stage. Do not worry about doing too much damage. Depending on the thickness of the pulp, the paper may take three or four days to dry.

16 Should you want the paper to have a smoother surface, simply roll it flat while slightly damp with a rolling pin, but do not press too hard or the paper might tear.

17 After pressing, allow the sheets to dry separately under heavy weights.

Allowing paper to dry

Fiber Length

Most paper can be recycled, but the kind that contains long fibers works best. To check the length of the fibers of the paper you want to use, tear a sheet in half. If it has long wispy ends, it will work well.

◆ *The following projects involve making paper: Flora and Fauna Fun (page 36), Trippin' Triptych (page 64), Circle of Fun (page 101), and Glitter Christmas (page 129). Of course, you can always make your own paper for any card creation.*

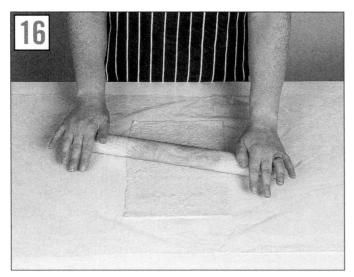

Rolling paper until flat and smooth

Duo Paper

Duo paper or plastic wrap laminating is a great technique for many projects including journals, portfolios, origami boxes, and of course greeting cards! Dyed papers (see the Dyed Paper technique on page 23) are perfect when used in combination with this technique.

 Get Started:

lightweight handmade papers • plastic wrap • iron

1 Take two very distinct lightweight papers. Good choices are inexpensive tissue paper, lightweight handmade paper, or any uncoated text-weight paper. Lay the plastic wrap on the backside of the first paper. Layer the second paper (with the good side up) over the plastic wrap.

2 Using a warm iron, press the two pieces together firmly. This may require a few test runs because irons and wrap vary.

3 Fold the paper in half as soon as possible. This makes the crease very crisp.

Remember: The less expensive the wrap, the better. Also, if the papers you choose are very thin, you can layer smaller die-cut paper pieces in between the two layers.

◆ *The Trippin' Triptych on page 64 utilizes the Duo Paper technique.*

Sculpture Paper

For this particular technique, gesso is used. Any scrap paper, thin junk mail, newspaper, newsprint, paper towel, napkins, bath tissue, wrapping tissue, or bond paper can be used. Let's get going!

 Get Started:

paper towel • kitchen foil • white gesso • foam brush • Diamond Glaze and PearlEx or any art medium: watercolor, acrylics, or inks • black acrylic paint • hair dryer

Switch It Up

Plain newsprint gives a smooth appearance, while paper towels give a fuzzier texture. Try using a plain paper table napkin because it gives the look and feel of canvas when you're done.

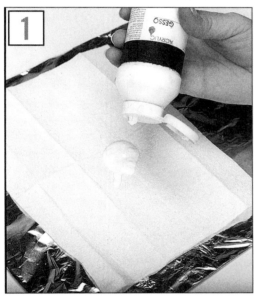

1 Place the paper towel in the center of the foil. Pour a 1"-wide dollop of white gesso in the center of the paper towel.

2 Using a foam brush, spread the gesso. Moving any liquid paint, gesso, or medium is always more effective if spread from the center of the project paper outward.

Continues

3 Go over the edges of the towel. Let it dry completely before continuing.

4 You can apply almost any art medium including acrylic paints, inks, and watercolor paints to this base paper. Here, a combination of Diamond Glaze and PearlEx is being used. The ratio of PearlEx to Diamond Glaze can vary. It is suggested that you start at four parts Diamond Glaze to one part PearlEx. Gradually add more powder for a more opaque paint.

5 Apply the first color thoroughly over the gesso. Let it dry completely before continuing.

6 Crumple the base paper. Lay it out flat. Using a foam brush, mix a teaspoon (5 ml) of Diamond Glaze with ¼ teaspoon (1 ml) of black acrylic paint. Brush this mixture lightly over the cracks of the paper.

7 To speed up the drying time, use a hair dryer. Do not use a heat gun for this process—it could make the paint bubble.

◆ *This technique is found in the Picture Pebble project on page 80.*

Dyed Paper

All you need are some paper towels and dye, and you're ready to go!
Wrap the dyed paper over pieces of chipboard and you'll create lovely
accents fit for any card!

 Get Started:

> plastic or latex gloves • small cups or bowls • water •
> several colors of dye ink • two-ply paper towels • metallic
> ink or paint

Don't Forget: When handling any type of dye, it's a
good idea to protect your hands with plastic or latex gloves.

1 First, put each dye or stain color in its own bowl.

2 Add five drops of dye or ink to two tablespoons of water.
The dye should appear darker in the bowl than the
desired color.

Switch It Up

*If you would like to have a
more metallic cast for your
papers, add a few drops of
acrylic metallic inks (the
type calligraphers use).*

Continues

23

Switch It Up

If you have a very light-colored piece, stamp it with a large background stamp.

3 Fold a towel into a small square, then dip the corners into the different-colored dyes. Folding the towel like a fan will give you a different pattern.

4 Once the colors have bled together, allow the piece to dry completely.

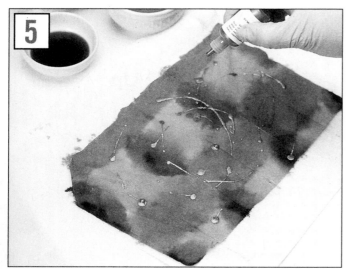

5 Sprinkle metallic ink or paint over the paper surface for a splatter effect. Create several different-colored sheets using this technique. Let the paper dry overnight.

◆ *See Dye Hard on page 116 to use this technique in a card project.*

Elements: Getting Started, Switching It Up, and Extra Credit

There are certain components that you will find throughout the book to aid you in your craft adventures. These tidbits are here to give you the inside scoop about a particular project you are working on, informing you of what you need do to make your craft look as it appears in the visuals, and other ideas for being imaginative with your creations.

In addition, quips of advice are splashed throughout the text to alert you to any issues that may involve supplies, tools, and the actual card-creating process. These advice blurbs are titled as *Remember* and *Don't Forget*. It is advised that you read these words of wisdom before you proceed with a project so that you get all of the information necessary to plan and create your crafts accordingly.

Get Started

This is what is commonly known as the materials section, where you'll find out what specific supplies are needed to create the card projects in this book.

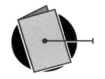

Switch It Up

You'll find this element throughout the book and find that it's like a little nudge to remind you to go wild when it comes to substituting supplies and materials. Try beads instead of crystals or use different paint colors than the ones used in the project directions. You *don't* have to follow the suggestions given in "Switch it Up"—feel free to make up your own alternatives!

Extra Credit

Some projects in this book have been labeled as extra credit. This means that although there are no difficult greeting card projects for you to choose from, there are some projects that are a little more involved. When you see a project labeled as extra credit, this is a heads-up that it might require that you know a particular technique or two or that you might need extra time to complete the card.

Don't be afraid to try a project when you see it labeled as extra credit. Though these projects might have more steps or require a little more concentration, they're just as fun to create as the other cards in this book. So go for it—you may realize that the extra credit means extra fun!

Hopefully you'll use these different book elements to your advantage as you craft card after card. **Enjoy!**

Part Two

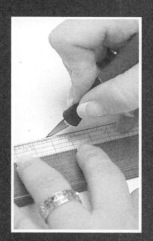

Get Creative:
Cards for Everyone You Know

Corset Creation

This card is just like a present—you get to open it by pulling on the fancy ribbons, fibers, and charms.

Get Started:

2 large shipping tags • scissors • assorted punches • green metallic pigment ink • silver leafing pen • rubber stamp • purple and dark green inks • vellum • Diamond Glaze • craft knife • sheer ribbon • cardstock • doublestick tape • charms

1 Cut two large shipping tags into a triangular shape.

2 Punch out a variety of shapes, which will create a lacy effect on the tags.

Remember: Punch larger shapes first, then fill in with punches of decreasing size.

3 Rub green metallic pigment ink over the tags.

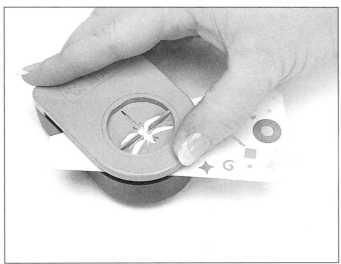

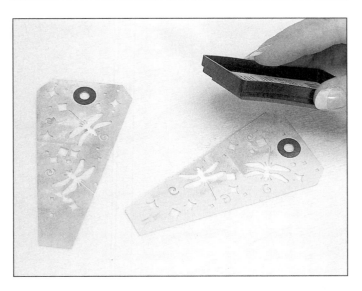

Continues

4 Using a silver leafing pen, color the reinforcements and edges. Use the pen to add a few drops, drips, and streaks.

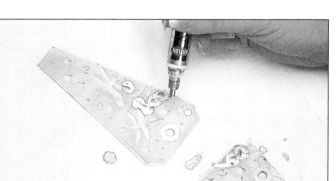

5 For the underpinning of the corset, stamp a piece of coordinating vellum with purple and dark green inks. Use a few drops of Diamond Glaze to adhere the tags to the vellum.

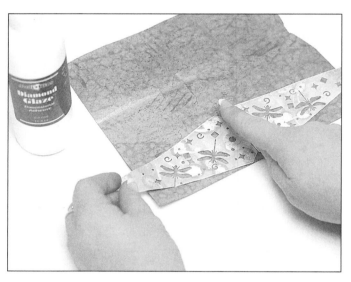

Remember: Score the tags with the backside of your craft knife. This creates a very sharp crease.

6 Trim away any extra vellum.

7 Mark the tags where they will fold around the cardstock. Score the vellum side of the tags so they will easily fold.

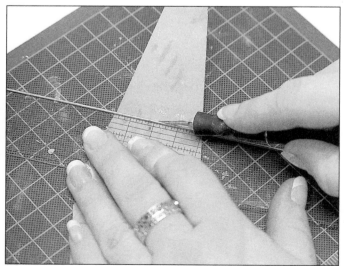

8 Trim out the holes in the tags.

9 Thread a piece of sheer ribbon through the holes.

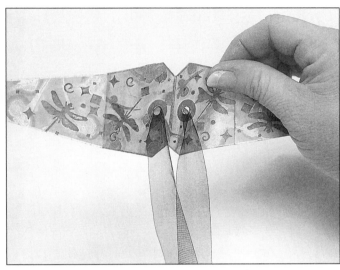

Don't Forget: A corset can be made to open in the front by cutting the front seam with a craft knife.

10 Wrap the corset around the cardstock. Secure the corset with doublestick tape.

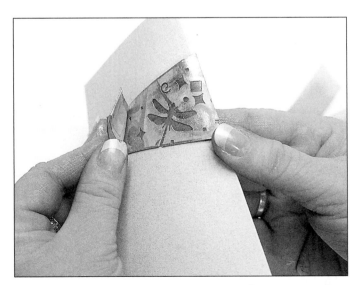

11 Add a large silver charm or bead. The card should be opened by sliding the whole corset up over the top.

Mini Message

These cards fit perfectly with the cute little envelopes you can make in this book on page 9 (Basic Envelope Templates). Jazz up your card to make it look sassy!

Get Started:

brown paper (text weight) • pencil • scissors • bone folder • small round stamp • rectangular stamp • word stamp • craft knife • white glue • round gift tag • black and green dye inks • metallic pigment ink • metallic embossing powder • heat gun • tall notecard • gold thread • double-sided tape

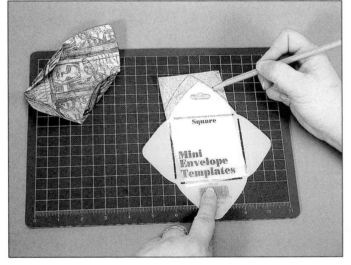

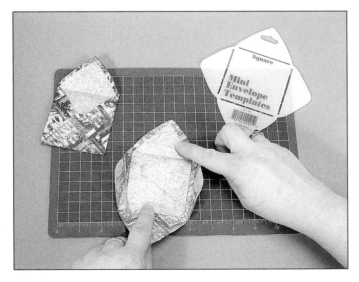

1 Stamp plain brown lightweight paper with black dye ink. Trace the mini square envelope template and follow the Basic Envelope Template instructions on page 9. Score card using bone folder. Cut out envelope and set aside.

2 To make a liner for the envelope, use a pencil to trace the square interior through the template slots. Continue tracing around the top flap. Cut along the pencil lines.

3 Trim ¼" off the liner on all sides. Glue the liner to the inside of the envelope. Glue the seams of the envelope and set aside.

Continues

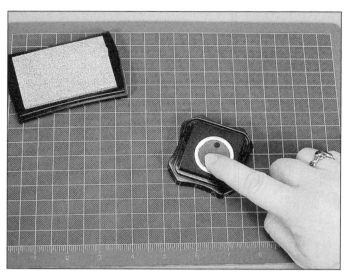

4 Color the tag with dye ink. Wipe off any excess ink on the metal rim of the tag. Allow to dry completely according to the manufacturer's directions.

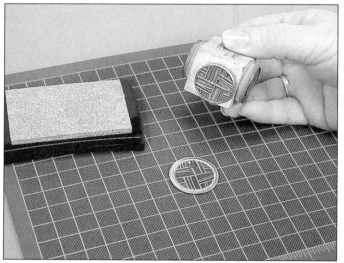

5 Stamp a design on the tag with pigment ink. Wipe away any excess on the rim with a paper towel.

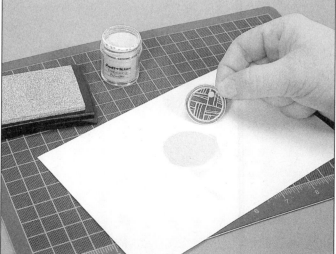

6 Sprinkle embossing powder over the wet pigment ink. Shake off any excess.

7 Use a heat gun to heat the embossing powder until it melts.

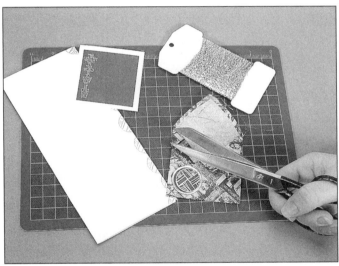

8 Using the template on page 11 from the Basic Envelope Template, trace just the inside square and cut it out. Trim this piece as necessary to fit inside the envelope perfectly. Write or stamp your message on the card and slip it in the envelope. Wrap gold thread around the envelope several times and tie on the tag. Trim away any excess thread with scissors.

Remember: Raffia, yarn, and narrow ribbons also work well for trims on greeting cards. Be sure to keep the size of the trim in proportion to the card.

9 Attach the envelope to the card. If you would like, stamp the tall notecard along the edge with a coordinating design. Apply the piece to the front of the card with any double-sided tape.

Extra Credit

Flora and Fauna Fun

Handmade paper, dried flowers, twigs, and raffia have been used to make these natural-looking cards, envelopes, and tags. Decorated with fruit, butterflies, and ladybugs cut from handmade paper, they are sure to be a hit with anyone who enjoys nature and the countryside.

Get Started:

pencil • ruler • handmade paper: dark green, light green, natural, light blue, red, mustard yellow, mauve, terracotta, cream, light brown • water • straight edge • tacky glue • light card, brown • scissors • craft knife • cutting mat • twigs, cinnamon sticks, dried flowers, bark, straw • hole punch • natural raffia, open-weave hessian • permanent marker pen, black • craft wire, thin

Pineapple Card

1 Using a pencil and ruler, draw a rectangle 6" × 10" onto terracotta handmade paper (see page 14 to review how to make paper).

2 Fold and dampen the paper along the pencil lines. Using a straight edge, tear off the rectangle. This will give the edges a natural torn finish.

3 Tear a rectangle of natural color paper 3½" × 4⅛". Glue the rectangle onto the center front of the card.

4 You can buy the pineapple paper ready-made, but if you're making your own: Cut two pieces of thin hand-made paper in cream and light brown, 6" × 8".

5 Take the light brown piece and draw a rectangle ⅜" in from the edges using a pencil and ruler.

6 Mark off ¼" intervals along the short sides of the rectangle.

7 Using scissors, cut parallel slits within the rectangle, joining the marks together on both sides.

8 Cut strips of cream paper, ¼" wide and 6" long.

9 Weave one color's strips up in between the strips of the other color, forming a basket weave effect. See Figure 1.

10 Trace the pineapples, NOT the pineapple tops, on page 38.

11 Using scissors, cut out the shapes and lay them onto the basket weave paper.

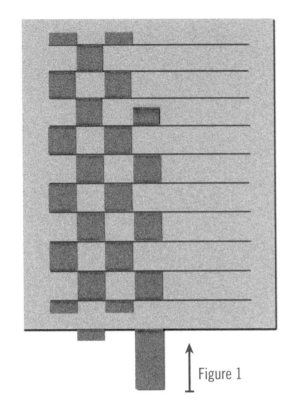

Figure 1

12 With a pencil, draw around the outside edge of the pineapples, and then cut around the edge.

13 Once you have cut out the basket weave pineapples, you may need to apply a small amount of glue to the edges of the paper strips to hold the pineapples together.

14 Trace the pineapple TOPS from page 38.

15 Cut the larger tops from dark green paper and the smaller insides from light green.

16 Cut two narrow strips of dark green paper to go down the center of the tops. Refer to the photo as a guide.

17 Glue both pineapples, both tops and bottoms, onto the front of the card.

18 Cut three lengths of twig or cinnamon stick 2⅜" long, and glue these on both sides of the pineapples and on top of the card.

Continues ➤ **37**

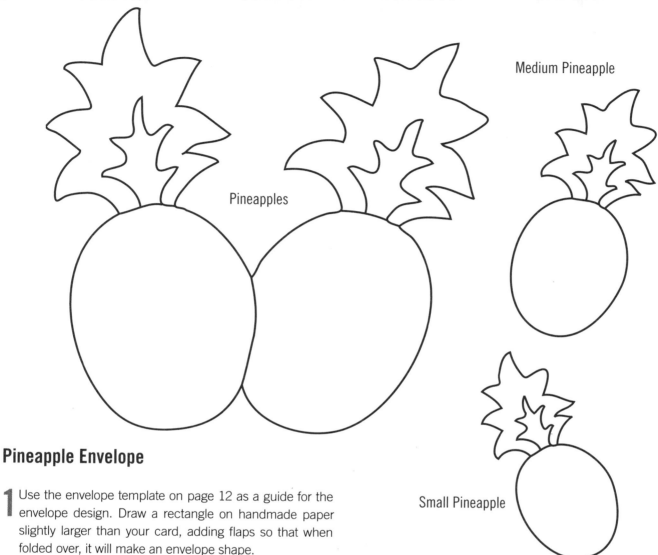

Medium Pineapple

Pineapples

Small Pineapple

Pineapple Envelope

1 Use the envelope template on page 12 as a guide for the envelope design. Draw a rectangle on handmade paper slightly larger than your card, adding flaps so that when folded over, it will make an envelope shape.

2 Use scissors to cut out the envelope, then score and fold on the dotted lines. See next page.

3 Fold the side flaps in, and the bottom up, and use glue to keep the envelope together.

4 Tear a piece of handmade terracotta paper 2" × 2⅜" and glue this to the top left-hand corner of the envelope.

5 Tear a slightly smaller piece of natural color paper and glue this to the center of the terracotta paper.

6 Trace the small pineapple figure, and create the bottom from the basket weave paper and the top from dark and light green paper, as you did with the pineapple card.

7 Glue the complete pineapple over the rectangle of hand-made paper in the corner of the envelope.

Pineapple Gift Tag

1 Tear a piece of terracotta paper 2¾" × 3½" and make a hole in one corner of the paper using a hole punch.

2 Tear a piece of natural color paper 2" × 2½" and glue it to the center of the terracotta paper.

3 Cut the bottom of the pineapple from basket weave paper and the top from dark and light paper, using the figure below.

4 Glue the pineapple to the tag. Thread the tag with a length of raffia.

Apples

Small Apple

Apple Card

1 Tear a rectangle 6" × 10" of green handmade paper. Score and fold the card in the same way as for the pineapple card.

2 Tear a rectangle of natural color paper 3¼" × 4¾" and glue it to the center front of the card.

3 Cut a piece of thin flat bark or ridged brown paper 3¼" × 4". Glue it over the natural color paper.

4 Make a bow from several lengths of raffia and glue it to the top left-hand corner of the bark.

5 Use scissors to cut the apples and leaves from light green handmade paper. Cut the leaf veins from dark green paper. Cut the highlights on the apples in white.

6 Glue the apples and leaves onto the front of the card. Cut short lengths of twig or cinnamon stick for the stems, and glue them to the tops and bottoms of the apples.

Apple Envelope

1 Make an envelope in the same way as for the pineapple card (see at right), by adding a rectangle of green and natural paper, and a small apple. See the figure above for tracing the apple.

Apple Gift Tag

1 Tear a rectangle of natural color paper 2½" × 3¼".

2 Make the tag in the same way as for the pineapple tag, by adding a rectangle of green paper, and a small apple. Use the figure above to trace the apple for the tag.

Ladybug Card

1 Tear a rectangle 6" × 10" from gray paper. Score and fold the card in the same way as you did for the pineapple card.

2 Tear a rectangle of green paper 3¼" × 4" and glue it to the center front of the card.

3 Cut a clover leaf shape from light green paper using the figure on page 41.

4 Glue the clover leaf to the card, adding leaf veins in dark green paper.

5 Use the figures on page 41 to cut a large and a medium ladybug from red paper. Do not cut out the holes or details within the shape.

6 Glue the ladybugs onto the card; add spots, head, and tail markings, and feet using a black permanent marker pen.

7 Glue two small pieces of twig or cinnamon sticks in opposite corners of the card.

Ladybug Envelope

1 Make an envelope in the same way as for the pineapple card (see page 38).

2 Add a rectangle of green handmade paper, a small green clover leaf, and a small ladybug. Use the figures on page 41 for tracing.

Ladybug Gift Tag

1 Tear a rectangle of dark green paper 2¾" × 3¼".

2 Make the tag in the same way you made the pineapple tag, adding medium-sized and very small ladybugs as well as a small clover leaf. Use the figures on page 41 to trace the appropriate ladybug.

Small Clover Leaf

Large Clover Leaf

Clover Leaf

Very Small Ladybug

Small Ladybug

Medium Ladybug

Large Ladybug

Butterfly Card

1 Tear a rectangle 6" × 10" from mustard yellow handmade paper.

2 Cut a square of open-weave hessian 3½" × 4½" and glue it to the center of the card.

3 Use the figure below to cut a leaf from green paper.

4 Glue a length of thin craft wire onto the back of the leaf for the spine. Make vein marks on the leaf using a blunt tool.

5 Glue the leaf and a spray of dried flowers onto the hessian.

6 Use the figure below to cut a butterfly from mauve paper, the markings from dark blue, and a body from cream.

7 Use a dark blue pencil to add detail lines to the butterfly wings.

8 Glue the butterfly onto the card adding two lengths of straw for antennae.

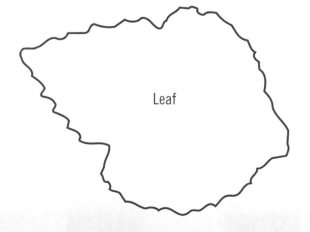

Leaf

Butterfly Envelope

1 Make an envelope in the same way as you did for the pineapple card, by adding a rectangle of yellow hand-made paper, and a small butterfly.

2 Use the figures below to trace the small butterfly for the envelope.

Small Butterfly

Butterfly

Butterfly Gift Tag

1 Tear a rectangle of yellow paper 2¾" × 3¼".

2 Make the tag in the same way you made the pine-apple tag, by adding a small rectangle of hessian and a small butterfly. (See above figure to trace small butterfly.)

Beatnik Terrific

Square cards are great for this project since the measurements will be the same all the way around.

 Get Started:

removable tape or doublestick tape • 2 identical cards • craft knife • transparent ruler • acetate • stamps • assorted paper for confetti • spiral punches • paper scraps • circle cutter • chenille yarn

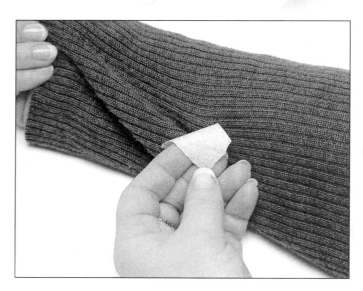

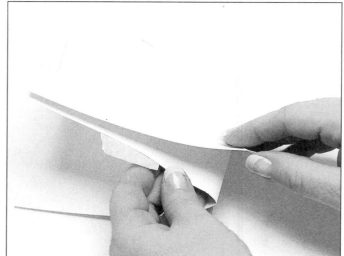

1 Take any kind of tape and place it several times on any fabric. This will create a surface on the tape that is not as sticky.

2 Begin by taping the two identical cards back to front.

3 Using your craft knife and a transparent ruler, cut a ½" frame out of the taped section. You should be cutting through two pieces of cardstock, so be sure to have a fresh blade in the knife.

Remember: With any type of tape try not to stretch it taut, as it will pull back to its original size, causing a bubble in the tape and paper.

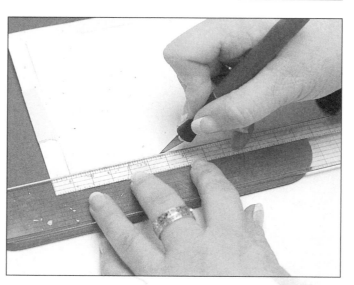

4 The frame should match up perfectly when you put the finished card together.

5 Apply clear doublestick tape around one of the frames.

6 Cut two pieces of acetate about 5" square and 4¾" square for inside the frame. (The smaller piece creates a pocket of acetate so that you will not need as much tape.) Place the larger piece of acetate on the frame that has been taped.

Remember: You can use countless things for the inside of the acetate pocket. Try confetti, stickers (back-to-back), tiny beads, glitter, or colored mica chips.

7 Stamp two identical images. Using doublestick tape, adhere the images back-to-back. Lay these images and other elements on the acetate.

8 Here punches were used to create confetti from leftover paper scraps. Make sure the paper you are punching looks good on both sides, and try to keep all of the materials in the center of the acetate as they tend to gravitate toward the exposed tape.

9 Sandwich your smaller piece of acetate over the tape. A small strip of tape should still be exposed.

10 Line up the inside edges of the second frame. Lay the top frame onto the tape.

Remember: Keeping white cardstock clean is often difficult. Keep a white rubber eraser and craft knife nearby for quick cleanups. Lightly scrape smudges with the knife, then even out the paper surface with the eraser.

11 Trim any excess tape, acetate, or cardstock from the outside edges of the card with a craft knife.

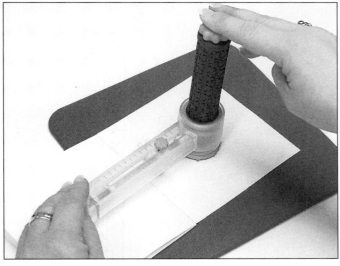

12 On the front panel of the card (which can be left solid) the artist created a large circle frame with a cutter.

13 To add color, tie on some chenille yarn.

Bead Intrigue

Beads are a quick way to spruce up any card. The way you can interchange the tiles with beads is overwhelming! Be sure to play around with the various colors and textures beads can offer to get the most exciting look from your card.

Get Started:

scissors • 15 or more shrink plastic tiles • heat gun • stamps of your choice • heavy chipboard • tray or box lid • Diamond Glaze • glass beads • double-sided masking tape • square notecard

1 Cut small squares of white shrink plastic into various sizes. Shrink the pieces with a heat gun until they become flat.

2 Quickly impress a stamp image into the hot plastic. Make up several of these pieces before moving on to the next step.

3 Place a 3½" × 3" piece of heavy chipboard in a small tray or box lid. Spread a thick layer of Diamond Glaze over the chipboard.

Continues

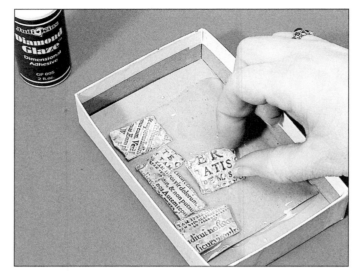

4 Arrange the tiles in an attractive pattern on top of the glaze. Leave space between each tile.

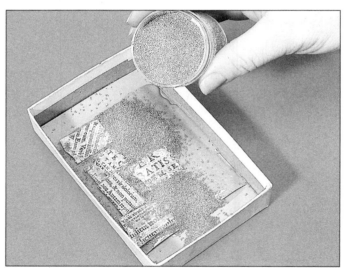

5 Pour glass beads over the glaze. Leave the tray undisturbed for at least 20 minutes.

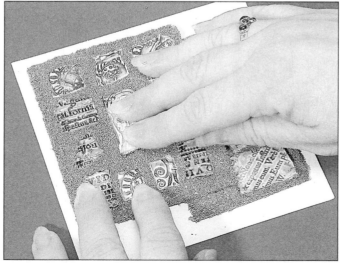

6 After the 20 minutes has passed, shake off any excess beads. Apply the double-sided tape to the chipboard. Layer the piece onto a square notecard. Layer two of these beaded pieces together for this project.

Remember: If the chipboard starts to curl after you have applied the Diamond Glaze, do not fret! As you press firmly into the tiles, the chipboard will relax.

Planting Greetings

This card can be framed and hung up as a year-round reminder of summertime. Give your gardener any of these creations to bring a bit of sunshine to his or her garden!

Get Started:

scissors • craft knife • cutting mat • ruler • cards: cream, light green, dark green, light blue, turquoise, and terracotta • white paper • ball-point pen • tacky glue • double-sided sticky tape • self-adhesive sticky pads • dried flowers

Create Your Card

1 Cut a rectangle of pale card 6½" × 6¾". Draw a fine pencil line midway across the width of the card.

2 Score along this line using a straight edge and the back of a craft knife. Fold the card along the score line. Make the other card in the same way using a rectangle of pale card 9½" × 6¾".

3 Make a tracing of the large or small card designs (page 53) onto white paper using a ballpoint pen.

4 Place the tracing onto the front of the folded card and draw over the dotted lines, pressing hard enough to make indentations in the card.

5 Draw over the indentations with a pencil. Cut out the marked rectangle in the center of the card: This will be the window opening.

6 Use the tracing to cut a window frame from colored card. Glue the frame over the opening on the front of the card.

7 Make a tracing of the large or small canopy below.

8 Transfer the design lines onto the card, and cut out the canopy.

9 Score along the dotted line at the top, and then fold the tab over onto the reverse side. Make a crease along the lower dotted line.

10 Glue the tab to the card using double-sided sticky tape: The top of the canopy should be level with the card top. Attach the bottom edge of the canopy to the card using self-adhesive sticky pads.

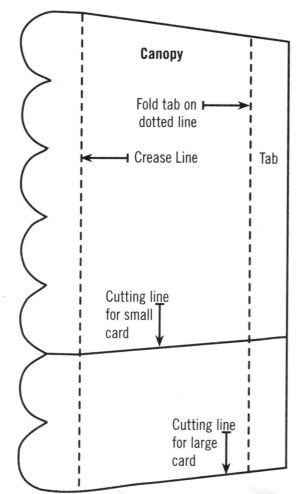

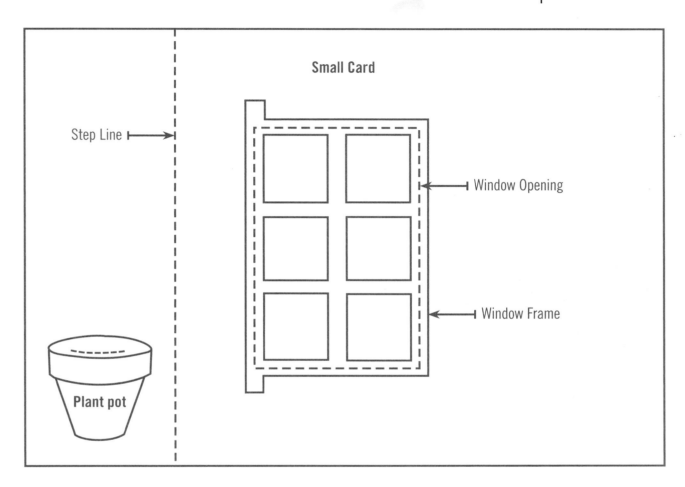

Small Card

Step Line

Window Opening

Window Frame

Plant pot

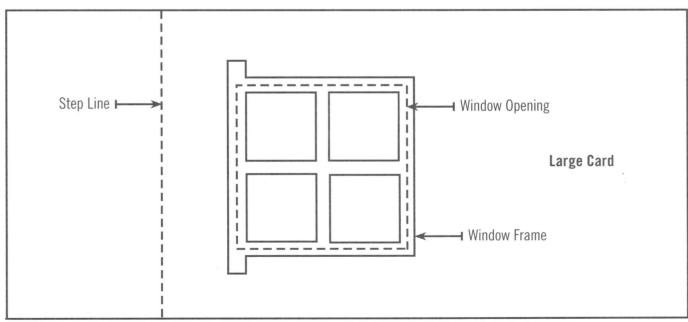

Step Line

Window Opening

Large Card

Window Frame

11 Make a tracing of the large or small steps on page 52.

12 Transfer the tracing to colored card, and cut out the steps.

13 Score along the dotted lines, then fold the top and bottom tabs over onto the back of the steps before folding along the remaining score lines to make steps.

14 Attach a row of self-adhesive sticky pads across the card, ½" below the pencil line drawn across the bottom of the card.

15 Use double-sided sticky tape to attach the top and bottom tabs on the back of the steps to the card, so that the top step is level with the pencil line and supported on the sticky pads.

16 Make a tracing of the plant pot and of the plant pot rim on page 53.

17 Use the traces to cut the pot and the rim from terracotta card.

18 Glue the rim onto the pot. Make a small slit in the pot just above the rim, which is shown as a dotted line on the diagram.

19 Cut the dried flowers into short lengths and insert the stems through the slit at the top of the pot.

20 Glue the stems onto the back of the pot. Make three pots for the smaller card, and five for the larger. Attach them to the steps using self-adhesive sticky pads, which will space them away from the card.

Post Your Hello

Send someone you care about this card made from old postage stamps—why not surprise a friend you haven't spoken to in a long while!

Get Started:

embossing ink • small tray • small dried flowers • paper towels • silver embossing powder • heat gun • cancelled postage stamps • double-sided tape • scissors • hole punch • thin gold thread • square notecard

1 Pour embossing ink into a small tray. Dip each flower into the embossing ink to coat.

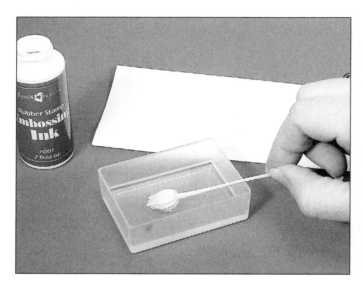

2 Blot each flower lightly to remove any excess ink.

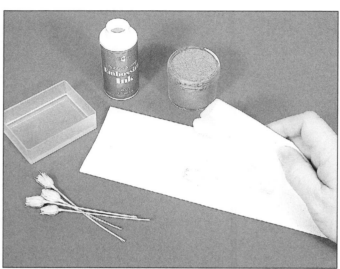

3 Coat the flowers in silver embossing powder.

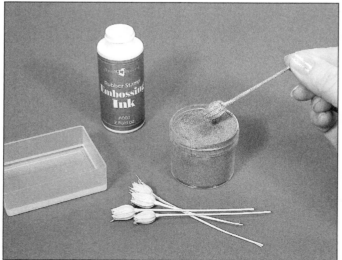

4 Heat the powder. If the flowers have long stems, and you decide to heat several at once, stick them into a stiff foam block. Don't get the heat gun too close to the foam or else it will melt.

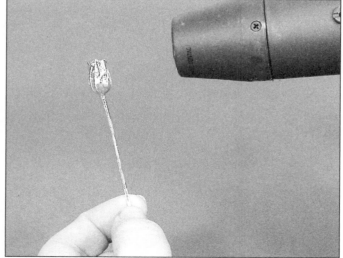

5 Set the flowers aside. Affix cancelled postage stamps to one side of double-sided masking tape. Trim the edges off using scissors.

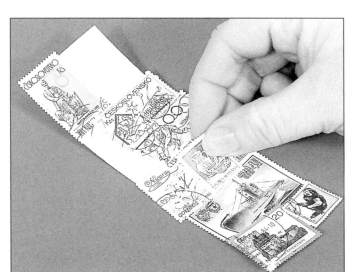

6 Punch two small holes about ¼" apart in the center of the tape.

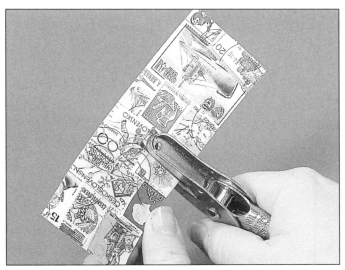

7 Tie on the silver-cup flowers using decorative gold thread.

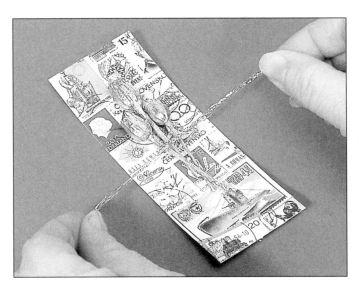

8 Remove the backing from the tape. Adhere the tape directly to a square notecard.

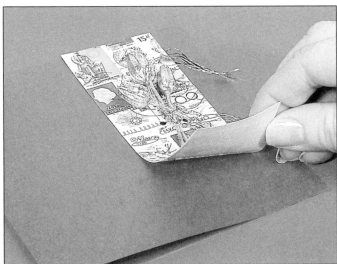

Celestial Creations

A perfect card for any occasion—or no occasion at all! Celestial cards, in silver or gold, are stunning and exquisite crafty gestures for friends, family, relatives, and acquaintances. Go crazy!

 Get Started:

triple-fold window cards: 3½" × 4½", 4½" × 3", 4¼" × 6" • holographic paper, blue • tacky glue • curling ribbon, gold • stationery stars • scissors • cards: silver, dark blue, white • watercolor paper • watercolor paint • container of clean water, paintbrushes • pencil • craft knife • cutting mat • marker pen, silver • corrugated card • ruler • cellophane, blue • holographic card, white • thick card • paper, dark blue • glitter pen, silver • thread, silver • tin cut from a single-portion cat food container • scrap card • fuse wire • knitting needle • glue gun • sun- and moon-shaped hole punch

Page 28

THE GREATEST THING IN THE WORLD IS TO KNOW HOW TO BE ES

Page 32

Page 36

Page 43

Page 48

Page
51

Page
55

Page
58

Page
62

Page
64

Page 70

Page 75

Page
80

Page
86

Gold Star Card

1 Cut a piece of blue holographic paper to fit behind the opening of a 3½" × 4½" window card.

2 Glue the blue holographic paper to the back of the window, inside the card.

3 Turn one flap of the card over onto the back of the holographic paper, and glue it in place.

4 Cut three lengths of gold curling ribbon approximately 4¾", 3", and 2¼" long.

5 Attach the three lengths of ribbon to the top right-hand corner of where the holographic paper meets the card using a gold stationery star.

6 Twist the longest length of ribbon into a spiral and secure the end to the bottom left-hand corner of the card using a gold star.

7 Twist the shortest ribbon into a spiral and attach it to the bottom right-hand corner with a star.

8 Twist the last length of gold ribbon and attach it in the same way, halfway up the left-hand side of the card.

Shooting Star Card

1 Cut a rectangle out of silver card, 4¼" × 6", score, and fold in half.

2 Roughly tear a piece of watercolor paper to fit on the front of the card. Use dark blue and purple watercolor paint to add more color to the paper. Leave it to dry as the instructions on the paint bottle indicate.

Star One
Star Two
Star Three
Star Four
Star Five
Star Six
Moon

3 Trace Star Five above. Use a craft knife and cutting mat to cut out the star shape from the paper, making a star-shaped stencil.

4 Lay your star stencil on the bottom left corner of the painted watercolor paper. Use a silver metallic pen to trace the star shape by drawing within the area of the stencil that has been cut away.

5 Draw three straight lines behind the star using the metallic pen and a ruler.

6 Glue the watercolor paper to the front of the card.

Using a Metallic Pen

Before drawing lines on the front of your card, you must first check that the ink from your pen will not spread when applied to the surface of the paper. Practice drawing lines on scrap paper. The lines can be straight, dashed, dotted, or freehand. If you are using a ruler, make sure that it is turned on its concave side, or the ink may smudge when the pen is pressed against the edge of the ruler.

Continues

Corrugated Card

1 Cut a rectangle out of blue card, 4¼" × 6", score and fold in half as you did with the Shooting Star Card.

2 Draw a border around the edges of the front of the card using a silver marker pen.

3 Cut a piece of corrugated card 1¼" × 1½", and color it using a silver marker pen.

4 Use Star Five again to trace the star. Use the tracing to cut a star from corrugated card with a craft knife.

5 Color the star using silver marker pen. Cut a square of blue cellophane, ¾" × ¾".

6 Turn the card horizontally and glue the silver rectangle in the top left-hand corner of the card.

7 Glue the blue cellophane square toward the top left-hand corner of the corrugated card, with the silver star in the center.

Five Stars Card

1 Cut a blue rectangle of card 4¼" × 6", score and fold in half as you did with the Shooting Star and Corrugated Cards.

2 Draw a rectangle on the front of the card using a silver glitter pen and a ruler (see sidebar "Drawing an Outline" on this page).

3 Trace Star Five and transfer the star to white card. Cut out the star from the white card using a craft knife and cutting mat.

4 Using a silver glitter pen, color the star. Cut a square of thick card small enough to fit behind the glitter star.

5 Glue the star-shaped card onto the back of the glitter star. Then glue the star in the top left-hand corner of the card.

6 Make stencils of the other stars (page 59).

7 Use the stencils you just made to draw Stars One to Four in silver marker pen, in a straight line, radiating down from the glitter star glued in the top left corner of the card.

Drawing an Outline

A metallic pen can be used to outline a window opening, or to add a border to the card. Choose a pen with a fine tip. Shake the pen well, and then make straight, dotted, or dashed lines on the card. Draw in freehand, over a pencil line, or use a ruler or straight edge for guidance.

Hanging Star Card

1 Cut a piece of dark blue paper to fit behind the opening of a 4¼" × 6" window card. Outline the opening of the card with a line of silver glitter.

2 Trace Star Six. Use the tracing to cut out two star shapes from silver holographic paper.

3 Using your silver glitter pen, outline around the edges of both stars.

4 Cut two lengths of silver thread: one piece 2" long, the other 3¼" long. Glue a piece of thread to the back of each star.

5 Glue the ends of the thread inside the card, so that the star hangs down in the window.

6 Glue a piece of dark blue paper over the opening in the card, and fold the paper under the borders of the card. Then glue the card together.

7 Add small spots of glitter glue to the blue paper in the card's window.

Tin Star Card

1 Cut a rectangle of silver card 4¼" × 6". Score and fold in half as you did with the Five Stars Card.

2 Tear a rectangle of dark blue paper to fit onto the card. Glue it at an angle to the front of the card.

3 Trace Star Six and use it to trace onto tin sheeting.

Remember: You can use a small cat food tin if you can't find tin at your local craft shop.

4 Put the tin star on a scrap of thick card, then use a pencil to draw a pattern of dots and lines on the back of the star, making indentations in the tin. See Figure 1.

5 Cut a piece of fuse wire 4" long. Wind the wire around a knitting needle to make a stretched coil spring.

6 Use a hot glue gun to glue the spring to the back of the star. Then glue the star to the blue paper on the front of the card.

Tin Moon Card

1 Cut a rectangle of silver card 4¼" × 6", score and fold in half as with the Tin Star Card.

2 Cut a piece of dark blue paper slightly smaller than the front of the card.

3 Glue the paper in the bottom right corner of the card, so that there is a wider border at the top and on the left.

4 Trace Star Five and the moon, and use the traces to cut out shapes from tin.

5 Place the tin shapes of the star and moon face-down on a scrap piece of card and use a pencil to make indentations on the tin star, and to draw a face on the moon.

6 Glue the star and moon on the front of the card using a glue gun.

7 Use a sun- and moon-shaped hole punch to make five suns and four moons from dark blue paper.

8 Glue them onto the borders on the front of the card with tacky glue.

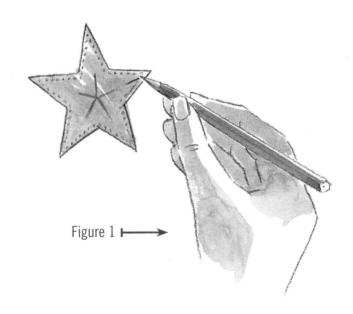

Figure 1 ⟼

Wonder Women

Why not create this card for a woman who you admire, care for, or wish you could hang out with more? She'll appreciate it.

 Get Started:

stamps of women • gold embossing powder • Kraft cardstock, brown • craft knife • dye re-inkers • Diamond Glaze • small plastic tray • small paintbrush • white colored pencil • doublesided masking tape • paper cords • tall notecard

Remember: Overglazing means to mix Diamond Glaze with dye re-inkers to use as a translucent paint.

1 Stamp and emboss an image in gold on brown Kraft cardstock. This image from the stamp used here is long, so cut it into three separate images.

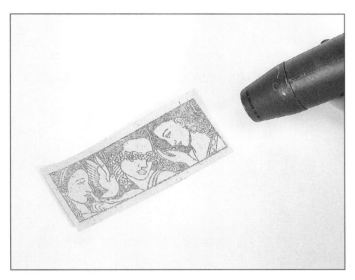

2 Mix one drop of each color dye with five drops of Diamond Glaze in a paint tray or small plastic dish. Paint the images, being careful to keep the glazing mixture off the gold embossing. The dove in the second section should be white, so a white pencil was used.

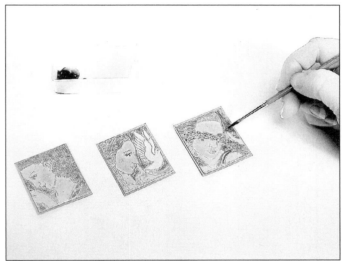

3 While the pieces are drying, create the border strip by cutting a piece of double-sided masking tape ½" wide and at least 8½" long. Cover the tape with paper cord, starting at the center and working outward.

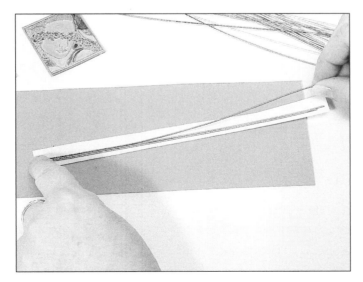

4 Attach the stamped images to the left side of the front of the tall card. Remove the liner from the tape and lay the border as shown.

Trippin' Triptych

For this duo paper project (see the Duo Paper technique on page 20), heavier papers should be used to accommodate the weight of decorations. Keep this in mind when creating your duo papers. Have fun and be creative with this "double-door" card style.

 Get Started:

pencil • cardstock • craft knife • plastic wrap • heavyweight handmade paper • iron • circle cutter • PearlEx • Diamond Glaze • rubber stamps • doublestick tape • round paper clips • assorted beads and charms • metallic thread • glass pieces • permanent black ink • wooden paper clips

1 Trace the template (on page 66) onto cardstock and cut out. Score the panels. Place a sheet of plastic wrap between the cutout triptych and your choice of hand-made paper. Trim away as much of the plastic wrap as possible.

2 Press your triptych shape with a warm iron (iron should be set on the silk setting). Trim away any excess plastic and paper.

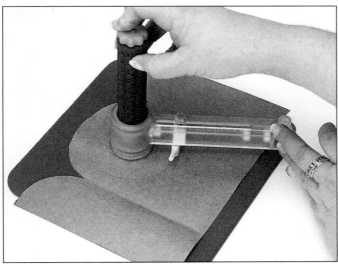

3 Using a circle cutter, remove a circle about 3½" from the center panel.

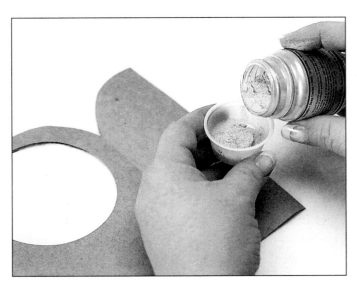

4 Mix about ½ teaspoon of PearlEx with 1 tablespoon of Diamond Glaze.

Continues

Trippin' Triptych Template

5 Scrunch a piece of plastic wrap to use as a texture tool. Dip the tool into the paint mixture and apply to the cardstock. Allow to dry for at least one hour.

6 Many rubber stamp companies sell unmounted rubber only. If you don't have time to mount rubber on wood, use a piece of doublestick tape to temporarily mount it to a stamp pad or small tin.

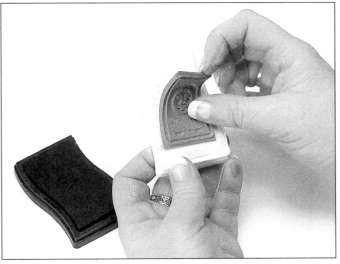

Remember: Triptychs are large cards. You can always create a smaller pattern to fit standard envelopes. When mailing, remember to check postal requirements for added weight, depth, height, and width.

7 Stamp and decorate the cardstock.

8 Embellish, embellish, embellish! Try using a round paper clip to hang a large stone bead with metallic thread.

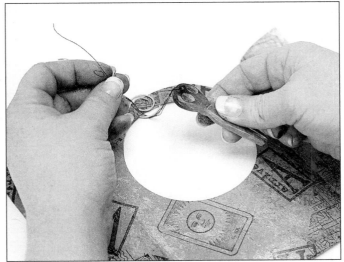

9 The charm used here is quite heavy, so an embellishment of equal weight will be needed to counterbalance the card when it stands. Try a small piece of stained glass whose edges have been sanded to give soft edges and an opaque finish. Any glass can be stamped with permanent black ink. To stamp an image on the glass, it is easier to lay the glass onto the stamp.

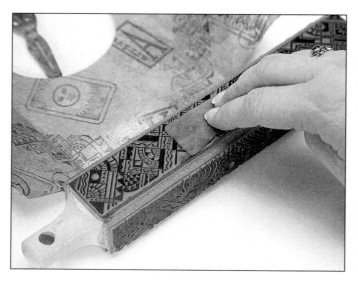

10 Add a small amount of Diamond Glaze to the back of the glass so as to keep it adhered to the paper.

11 Press firmly for a minute or weigh the piece down with a heavy book.

12 Once the glue has set, finish off the embellishments by adding wooden paper clips tied with threads or fibers.

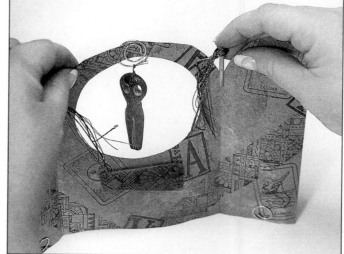

Part Three

Get Crafty:
Cards for Any Occasion

Crystal Memory

Show off a special memory with just the right picture of a friend, and use the beads and crystal to create a timeless look.

Get Started:

circle punch • cardstock • craft knife • 1/16" hole punch • three small brads • doublestick tape • watch crystal • tiny holeless beads • color-copied photo • Diamond Glaze • word stamp

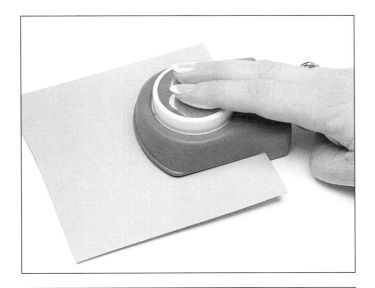

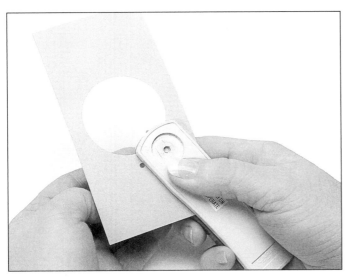

1 Punch a circle from a piece of cardstock. Push the punch in as far as possible.

Remember: Try punching wax paper to help paper punches work more smoothly.

2 Trim away any excess cardstock, leaving ½" on either side.

3 Punch three small circles along the top of the large circle, about ⅟₁₆".

4 Insert small brads into the tiny circles. Bend the prongs back tightly.

5 Check the front of the frame to be sure the prongs are hidden.

6 Using doublestick tape at the top and bottom of the frame only, apply the piece to the front of a tall card.

7 For added contrast, punch a 1" square from pale green cardstock. Apply doublestick tape to the back. Insert the square into the circle frame. Set aside.

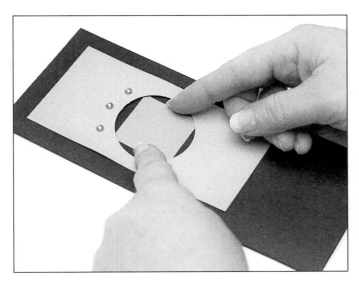

8 Dip the plastic watch crystal into the tiny holeless beads. Leave the crystal hollow side up on the table while you prepare the paper backing.

Remember: While the Diamond Glaze is still damp, pull the copy gently to flatten the surface before applying it to the rim of the crystal.

9 Use a color copy of an old photo as the backing to the crystal. Apply a small amount of Diamond Glaze evenly over the surface of the copy.

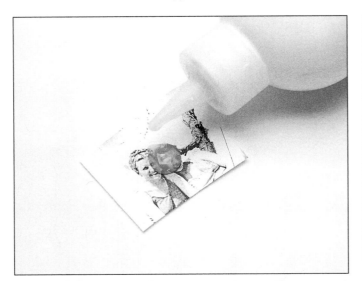

10 Allow the copy to dry for at least 30 seconds. Carefully apply to the rim of the crystal. Allow this piece to dry in this position for at least 20 minutes.

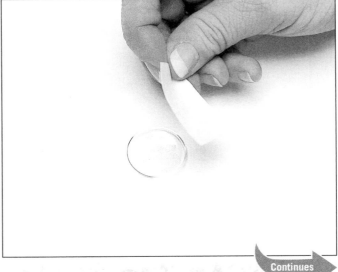

11 Trim any excess paper from the watch crystal edge.

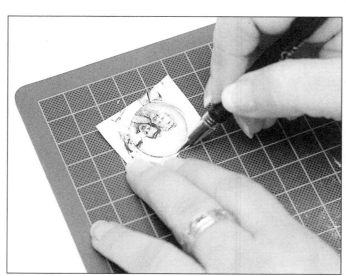

12 Apply doublestick tape to the back of the finished crystal. Attach the crystal to the card.

13 Use black dye ink and a small alphabet stamp to stamp a word along the bottom of the circle frame.

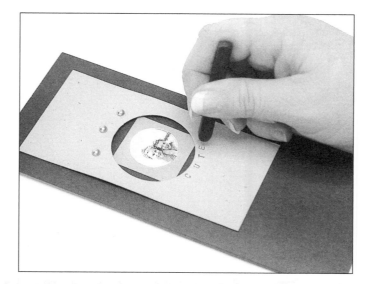

Mica Heirloom

There's nothing daintier than putting together the look of mica with photos. Perfect for the person whose photo you use, or to send someone a blast from the past—the possibilities are abundant.

Get Started:

circle cutter • craft knife • 2 square cards • mica tiles • 2 color-copied photos • doublestick tape • clear glue • dark green card • small metal alphabet • thin sheet of copper • scissors • small hammer • black ink • ⅛" hole punch • pencil • small brads

1 Using a circle cutter, punch, or craft knife, cut a 3" circle out of the center of a square card.

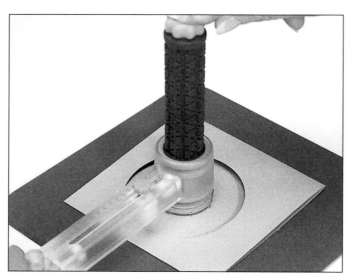

2 The circle should go through both sides of the card.

Remember: Make sure to color copy old black-and-white photos on the full-color setting to achieve the sepia-rich tones that heirloom photos have.

3 Carefully separate a mica tile into two thin equal pieces larger than the circle.

4 Cut two smaller circles out of identical color copies of an heirloom photo, about 2".

5 With a small piece of doublestick tape, attach the photos back-to-back.

6 Insert the photos between the mica tiles. Apply a drop of clear glue to an inconspicuous spot on the photo to keep the photo in place. With doublestick tape, attach the entire element to the inside of the card.

Don't Forget: Mica tiles can be tough to separate. Start with a thick piece, then separate it in half and then in half again until you achieve the desired thickness.

7 Seal the card.

Continues ➤ 77

Remember: On some of the other samples, two different color cards were used. With one card, the front was trimmed to achieve the ¾" border fold.

8 Trim a ¾" width of the scored fold from the folded dark green notecard.

9 Cut the second square card in half. You will use one of these halves to create the heirloom card's back panel. Place a section of doublestick tape on the inside of the dark green fold. Position the fold onto the framed photo and the back panel. Press firmly.

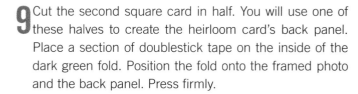

10 Metal alphabet stamps are available at most hardware and some stamp stores. They are simple to use with most metals, especially thin copper. Using scissors, cut out a small strip of copper.

Remember: When using an alphabet set to stamp a word, write out the word on a piece of paper the same size as the area to be stamped. Then set the paper above the area. Begin with the center letter and work your way out to each side.

11 Round off the corners with scissors.

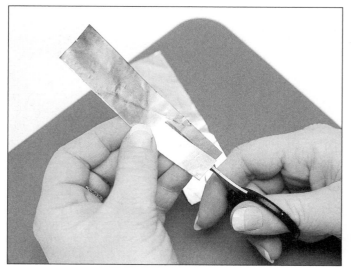
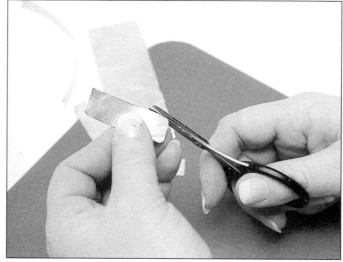

12 Holding each metal stamp straight on the copper strip, tap the top of the stamp several times with a small hammer.

13 After you complete the stamping, rub a bit of black ink over the stamped letters. Wipe off any excess from the copper.

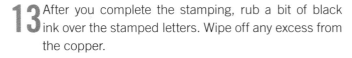
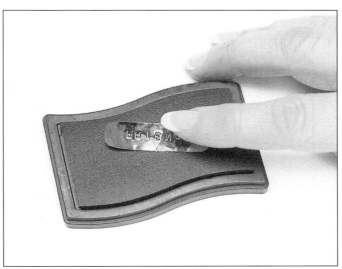

14 Punch a hole on either end of the copper strip with a ⅛" hole punch. Lay the strip on the front of the card for positioning. Mark the holes with a pencil, then punch corresponding holes in the cardstock.

15 Use tiny brads to hold the strip in place.

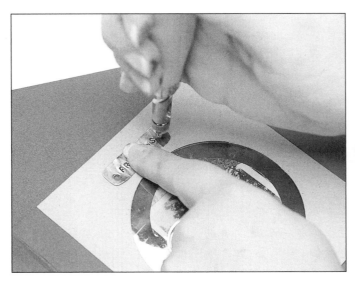
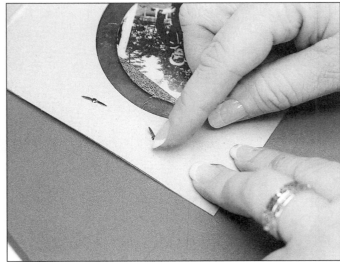

Picture Pebble

Perfect for small photos, magnify any design on your card with glass marbles! This project utilizes the Sculpture Paper technique on page 21.

 Get Started:

Diamond Glaze • PearlEx • foam brushes • acrylic metallic inks • hair dryer • sculpture paper • scissors • circle and square punches • craft knife • color-copied photo • picture pebble • transparent ruler • black dye ink • rubber stamp • doublestick tape • glue

1 Mix Diamond Glaze with a small amount of PearlEx or acrylic metallic ink.

2 Brush over the wrinkles with a foam brush. This artist painted half green and the other half gold.

3 Spice things up by drizzling inks or paints. Dry with a hair dryer to speed things up.

Switch It Up

Try rubberstamping the surface with acrylic inks for a more definite pattern. Some acrylic inks now come in pads, which makes them easier to apply to a stamp.

Continues ➤

4 Choose two contrasting pieces of sculpture paper. Cut a circle out of each color about 1½" in diameter. Place them together foil to foil.

5 Roll the edges together so that the lighter-color paper is on the inside. Mold the paper to form a small bowl.

6 Use a ½" circle punch to cut a circle from a copy of an old photo.

7 Pour into the bowl a pea-size dollop of Diamond Glaze. Place the photo in the bowl.

8 Lay a picture pebble into the bowl.

Switch It Up
The pebble in the bowl makes an interesting magnet. Simply glue a magnet on its back.

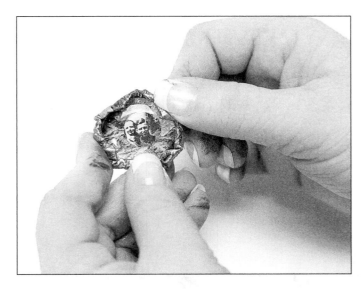

9 Crimp the edges of the paper around the pebble. Allow the piece to dry.

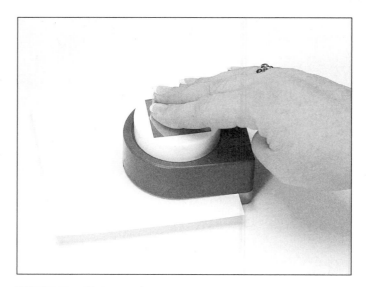

10 Punch out a 1½" square on white cardstock. Ideally you'll want a ¾" edge.

11 Use a transparent ruler to cut off excess from the other side.

12 To accent the two edges, use the same circle punch used on the photo to cut a half-circle.

Switch It Up

Using a small portion of a decorative punch along one of the edges of cardstock is a great way to add excitement to a card.

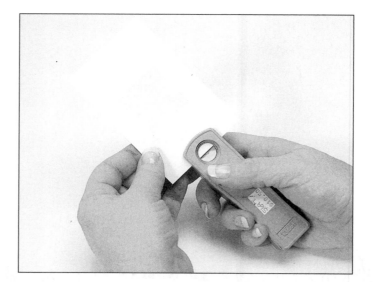

13 Using black dye ink, stamp several images or one large background stamp onto the cardstock.

14 Add a small piece of sculpture paper behind the cutout.

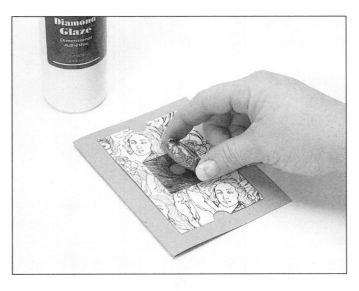

15 Assemble card with doublestick tape. Glue on the picture pebble.

Flower Power

Cheery, fun, and easy to make, these cards feel like spring and summer days with their bright colors and texture.

 Get Started:

corrugated card: red, yellow, purple • craft knife • cutting mat • ruler • paper: pink, red • deckle-edged scissors • spray adhesive • pencil • scissors • thin foam sheeting: yellow, pink, purple, blue, red, orange • ballpoint pen • white paper • tacky glue • hole punch • ribbon: blue, green

Purple Flower Power

1 Cut a rectangle of yellow corrugated card 8¼" x 8" using a craft knife and cutting mat. The corrugations should run vertical.

2 Using a straight edge and the back of a craft knife blade, make a score line halfway across the width of the card, using one of the corrugations as a guide.

3 Fold the card in half on the score line, lining up the edges of the card.

4 Cut a rectangle of pink paper 3" × 6¾" and decorate the edges using a pair of deckle-edged scissors.

5 Glue the rectangle of paper in the center of the front of the card using spray adhesive.

6 Trace the large flower and pot and diamond, using the figures below. Cut out each traced component from white paper.

7 Lay the traced flower onto thin purple foam, and draw around the edge using a ballpoint pen.

8 Cut out the purple foam flower using a craft knife and cutting mat. Then cut the other shapes from foam: use green for the stem, blue for the vase, and red for the flower's center and the seven diamonds.

9 Use deckle-edged scissors to cut a strip of orange foam to glue across the top of the pot.

10 Glue the flower, stem, and pot face-down onto the card so that the ballpoint pen lines do not show.

11 Glue the flower's center onto the flower, and the diamonds onto the pot.

Blue Flower Power

1 Use a craft knife and cutting mat to cut a rectangle 12" × 6" from purple corrugated card. Score and fold the card in half.

2 Cut a 4¾" × 4¾" square of red paper using deckle-edged scissors. Glue it in the center on the front of the card using spray adhesive.

3 Trace the small flower pot and diamonds below.

4 Lay the flower on the blue foam, and draw around the edge using a ballpoint pen. See Figure 1.

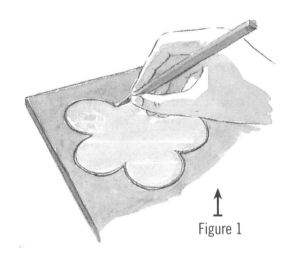

Figure 1

5 Cut out the flower using a craft knife and cutting mat. Then draw around and cut out the other shapes in the same way: green foam for the stem and leaves, pink for the flower's center and the six diamonds on the pot, orange for the leaf markings, and yellow for the pot.

6 Use deckle-edged scissors to cut a purple foam strip to glue across the pot.

7 Glue the flower, stem, leaves, and pot face-down on the card, so that the pen lines do not show.

8 Glue the flower's center onto the flower, and the diamonds onto the pot.

Large Flower and Pot

Small Flower and Pot

Flower for Tag

Diamond for Pot

Gift Tag

Flower Power Tags

1 Trace the gift tag on the left. Do not trace the flower within the tracing of the gift tag. Cut one tag from red corrugated card, and one from yellow. Use a hole punch to make a hole in the pointed end of each tag.

2 Trace the two different flowers and flower's centers below.

3 Cut one flower from yellow foam, and the other from pink. The centers should be cut from blue and orange foam.

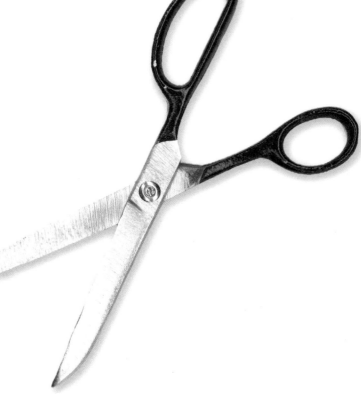

4 Glue the flowers and flower onto the tags.

5 Cut two lengths of ribbon 9½" long, one in green and one in blue.

6 Thread the ribbon through the holes in the tags.

Framed Gals

Send a friend a photo of the both of you—better yet, send it as part of this fun, shimmery card.

Get Started:

sculpture paper (see technique on page 21) • Diamond Glaze • PearlEx • pink iridescent ink • rubber brush • copy of photo • 1" × 1" piece of clear glass • ½" copper foil tape • craft knife • eyelets • eyelet tool • cardstock • small hammer • doublestick tape

Page 90

Page 94

Page
98

Page
101

Page
110

Page
105

Page
113

Page
116

Page
119

Page 126

Page 122

Page
129

1 Apply a layer of Diamond Glaze mixed with green PearlEx to the sculpture paper.

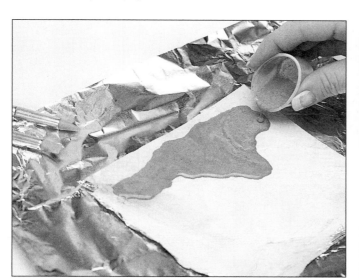

2 While the mixture is wet, use a rubber brush to create a pattern. Allow to completely dry.

3 Dip the rubber brush into the pink iridescent ink.

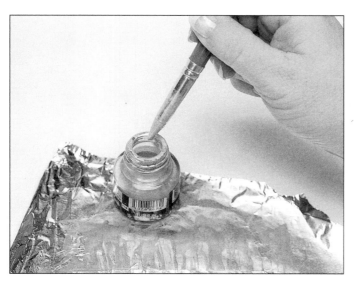

4 Paint pink iridescent ink into the pattern.

5 Place the piece of glass over the photocopy.

Remember: Most hardware stores will cut pieces of glass for you.

6 Crop the photocopy to the size of the glass.

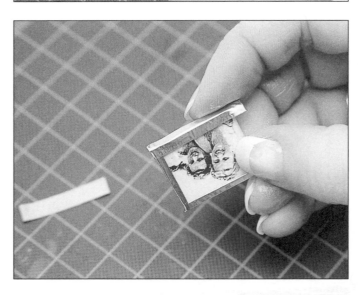

7 Foil tape is exceptionally sticky. Cut several 1" pieces of foil tape before you begin. Apply the foil, leaving an even, straight edge along the photocopy. Press firmly. Trim the foil as each side is applied.

8 With a craft knife, cut holes in the card for the eyelets.

9 Insert the eyelets through the sculpture paper and cardstock.

10 Use a hammer and setting tool to set the eyelets on the back of the card.

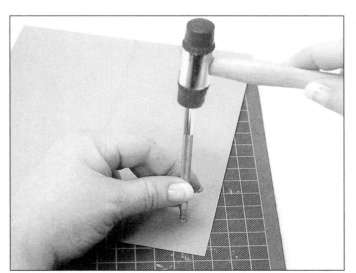

11 Adhere the photo to the card with doublestick tape.

Chinese Charm

Using charms and fabrics in cards yield a classy and elegant feel. Let your imagination help you out . . .

Get Started:

scissors • velvet • iron • rubber stamp • water • satin or silk fabric • fabric bond • cardstock • metallic thread • charm • doublestick tape

1 Begin with a small rectangle of good velvet. About 3" × 6" of rayon or acetate works best. Set the iron to the wool or cotton setting. Choose a stamp with a thick-lined pattern to it. A good choice is a bold stamp. Although the stamp is small, the line is heavy.

2 Flip the stamp and velvet over so that the backside of the fabric is facing you. Mist the back of the velvet lightly with water. Iron directly on the stamp for 10–15 seconds.

Switch It Up

Choosing a second piece of fabric will really make your card. For most heavy fabrics, leave the fabric with a raw edge. An exception is velvet because it frays.

3 Choose another piece of fabric. The piece shown here is only 2" × 3". Iron the bonding material to the fabric according to the manufacturer's directions on the package.

4 Remove the backing from the bonding material.

5 Position this fabric on the front of the velvet. Carefully iron the fabric to the velvet using the tip of the iron.

6 Iron the bonding material onto the back of the velvet. Do not overheat or you could lose the image you just pressed into the velvet.

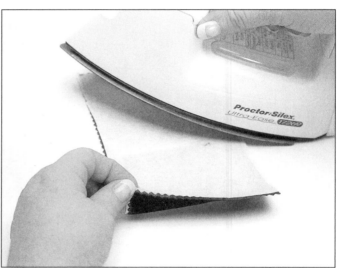

Remember: Some fabric scraps may be very uneven. Trimming them in an asymmetrical shape (as done here) can add interest. You may want to make a raw edge more intriguing by pulling a few threads, creating a ragged look.

7 Remove the backing. Place the piece onto cardstock cut to the desired size. In this case, it is about 5" × 3".

8 Fold over the raw edge. Iron down.

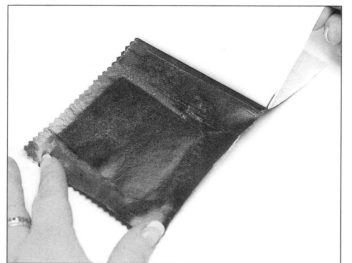

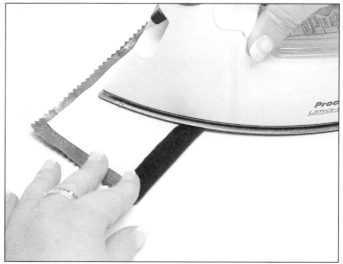

9 Press the completed piece with an iron once more, especially at the corners.

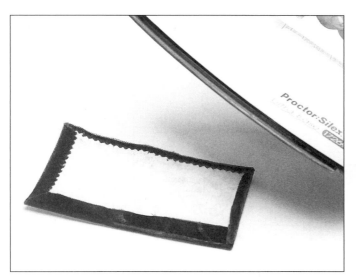

10 Create a loop with metallic thread. Tie on the brass charm.

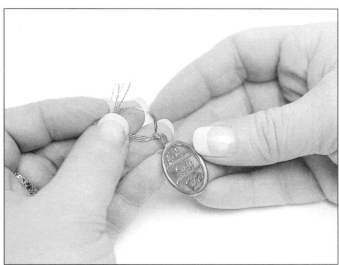

11 Attach the charm to the top left corner.

12 Add doublestick tape to the back of the piece. Place onto cardstock.

Doggy Diorama

Although the card might look complicated, the use of a template makes the whole process fast and easy. This one is perfect for dog lovers!

 **Get Started:**

11" × 17" cardstock in your choice of color • dog stamps • butterfly stamps • black dye ink • bone folder • pencil • craft knife • watercolor crayons or pens • double-sided masking tape • diorama template

1 Cut a piece of cardstock according to the size of your template. Stamp the characters in black dye ink. After the ink has dried completely, lay the template onto the paper and use a bone folder to score through the slots.

Remember: If you have a hard time holding the template and paper together, use removable tape to secure the two pieces, score them, then remove the tape.

2 With a pencil, mark the window area of the template.

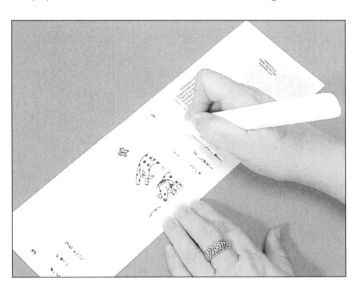

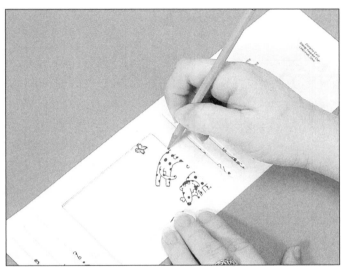

3 Now that you have marked where the window will be, you can add extra elements that will look as if they are coming out of the window. Try placing the stamp to make it look as if the dog is jumping halfway out of the window.

4 Cut out the window area with a craft knife. Be careful to cut around the designs stamped inside the window.

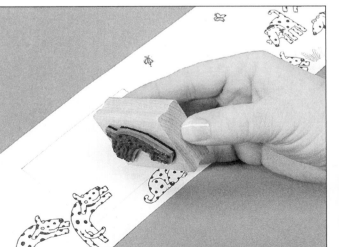

Continues

5 Crease each fold with the bone folder. Do not overwork the creases by folding back and forth. The card will stand better with crisp creases.

6 Check to make sure your card matches the photo below.

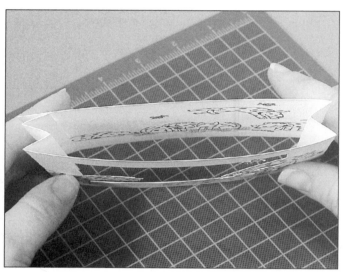

Remember: To add dimension to your diorama creation, use double-sided tape to adhere cutouts to the back of the diorama behind the window.

8 Apply double-sided tape to the side seam. Fold the entire card flat to seal it. Trim any uneven edges with a sharp knife—make sure to work slowly. Change your knife blade before making final trims.

7 Lay the entire card flat again. Add color to your design with colored pencils, markers, crayons, or watercolors.

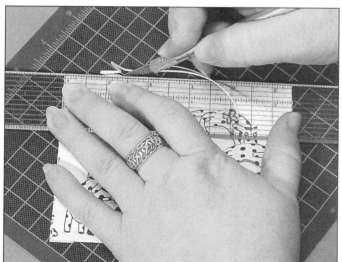

Circle of Fun

Experiment! Go wild with the charms—oh, and you don't have to use a circle, you can use any shape you want! This one's perfect for kids—or to make a friend smile . . .

 Get Started:

colored cardstock • chipboard (cardboard) • iron • fabric bond • assorted natural fibers • scissors • handmade paper • needle and thread • charms • doublestick tape

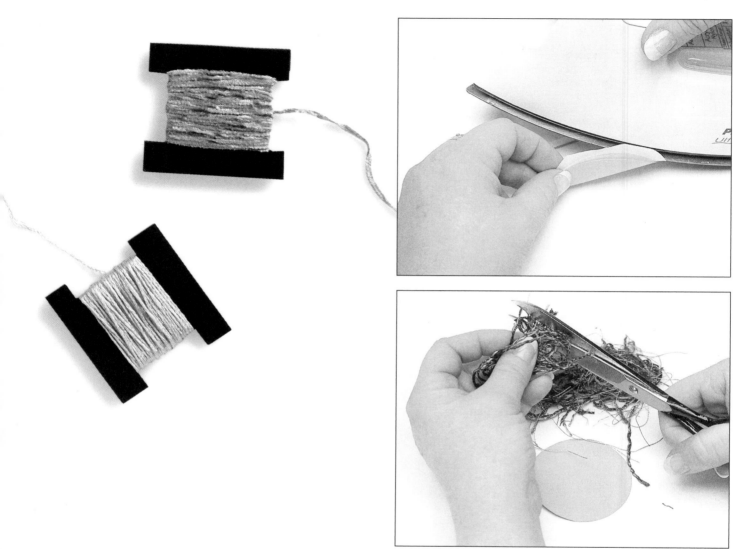

1 Using a round piece (or a shape of your choice) of cardstock or chipboard as a base, iron on a piece of bonding material. Remove the backing.

2 Cut the fibers into smaller pieces of varying lengths. Lay an assortment of the pieces onto the bonded side of the cardstock.

3 Use a hot iron to press. Check the fabric bond package directions to find out the right setting for the iron.

Remember: You will probably find that the fibers may not cover your cardstock completely. If this is the case, add small pieces of the bond to cover those areas. Then repeat the process.

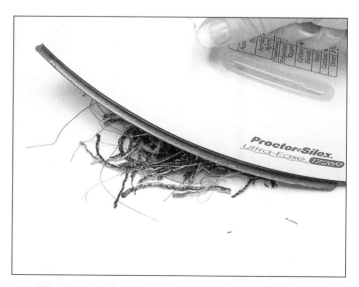

Don't Forget: Instead of trimming the fibers to the exact size of the cardstock, allow them to hang over for a raggedy look.

4 Turn the piece over to iron the cardstock side.

5 Leave a little edge when trimming. Even up the fibers. The edge of the cardstock should not be showing.

6 The background layer on this card uses coordinating handmade paper. Tear some of the edges to keep consistent with the ragged fiber element.

7 Add a few pieces of the bonding to the back.

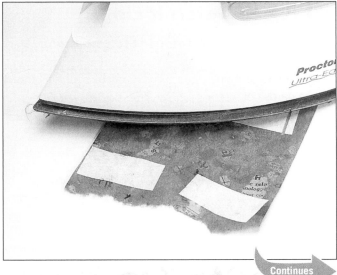

Continues

Switch It Up

The charms do not have to be in the shapes of hands and feet. You can use charms that represent those features. Try some small bells or beads instead.

8 Iron directly onto a piece of cardstock.

9 Sew on head, hands, and feet charms to create the character.

10 Adhere the fiber element to the card with double-stick tape.

Switch It Up

This card makes an excellent gift. Instead of permanently fixing the fiber element to the card, add a pin backing or a cord for a necklace. When creating jewelry, it is recommended that you use colored mat board as the base.

Time Flies

This card is perfect for when you want to just say "hello" or remind someone that you have been thinking about him or her.

 Get Started:

> fabric bond • assorted-color cardstock • heat gun • embossing powders • gold leaf • ROXS • charms or beads • metallic thread • doublestick tape • clear laminating sheet • stippling brush

1 Grab a few small pieces of fabric bond. Several small leftover pieces will work. Arrange the fabric bond on a circle of cardstock or art board. Melt the material with a heat gun.

2 Lightly sprinkle embossing powder over the entire surface.

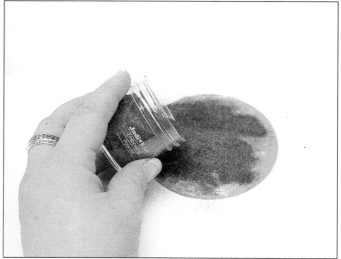

Switch It Up

Instead of embossing powder, try extra fine glitter or an assortment of tiny beads on the fabric bond.

Remember: String beads and charms before tying the thread to the card. Use a piece of tape on the end instead of making a bulky knot. It is easier to pull them exactly into position while wrapping.

3 Layer a few more pieces of fabric bond. Add another color of powder. Heat.

4 While the piece is warm, lay gold leaf over the edge area. Press firmly. Allow the piece to cool before removing the excess leaf.

5 Place a few more small pieces of bonding material on the center of the circle. Heat until melted.

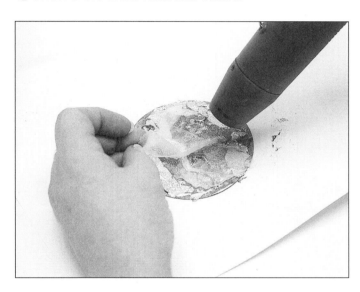

6 Pour on ROXS.

7 Place a charm and/or beads on metallic thread. Wrap the thread around the piece. Secure with doublestick tape.

8 Create the background layer with laminating sheets and gold leaf. Peel the backing from a clear laminating sheet.

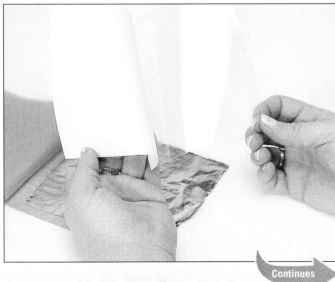

Remember: Using a box lid or plastic tray will catch the excess foil, which you can use again. Even the tiniest piece of foil can be used on another project. Don't worry if the foil folds over itself; the excess can be retrieved by softly brushing the surface.

9 Lay the laminating sheet sticky side up. Carefully lay the sheet of gold leaf on top of the laminate.

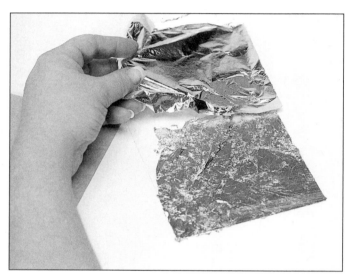

Remember: Some foil comes in small pieces contained in a box or bag. For this type of foil, it is strongly suggested you use a stencil or stippling brush to gently brush away the excess.

10 When using sheets of foil, your fingers can gently brush away the excess.

11 The technique of applying the foil to the laminate is much easier than using foil glues. With foiled laminate, you can use either side. If you like a matte gold finish, use the piece foil side up; if you want the surface to be extremely shiny, use the laminate side up. Either side can be placed on your card with doublestick tape.

12 Layer all the elements onto cardstock with double-stick tape.

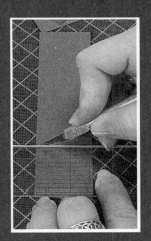

Part Four

Get Inspired:
Cards for Love

Pieces of Me

Everyone can create a mosaic card like this one. Not only is it one of the most elegant ways to create a greeting card, it is also one of the easiest and most beautiful projects you can make—anyone can do it. Try it!

 **Get Started:**

colorful, stamped, and unstamped scraps of paper • craft knife • cutting mat • double-sided masking tape • paper cording • cardstock • tall notecard

1 Use a craft knife to cut strips of colorful, stamped, and unstamped paper. Make sure the sides are all straight and parallel.

Remember: Try using two patterned or stamped papers for each mosaic—it makes for a much more interesting pattern.

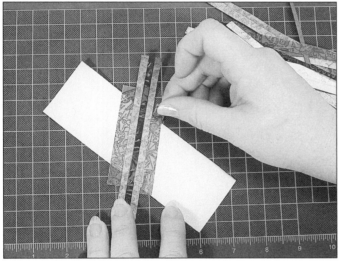

2 Start with a 4"-long section of double-sided masking tape. Lay the tape sticky side up on your cutting mat. Put one strip of paper at an angle across the center of the tape. Carefully lay another strip next to it, followed by another. Do not trim the strips at this time.

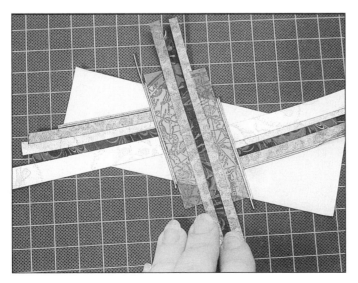

3 Lay a paper cord on either side of the strips. Press firmly. Once you have several strips across the center, begin laying strips perpendicular to your original strips.

Remember: It's best to use double-sided masking tape for this project because it is very forgiving. At times, you'll want to move the strips after you've put them on the tape. With this tape, you will be able to do so.

Continues

4 Repeat the process until the tape is covered.

5 When the tape is covered, turn the piece over with the backing face up. Trim ⅛" off each side of the tape.

6 Peel the liner off the tape and layer it onto cardstock. Trim the cardstock to about ½" around the mosaic. Apply double-sided tape to the back. Layer it all onto a tall notecard.

Remember: If you have tape showing between the strips, pour on a contrasting embossing powder to fill the spaces. Shake off any excess and heat. This not only fills in unwanted space, but it also gives a tile-like finish. You can also try coating the entire piece with a clear powder like Amazing Glaze.

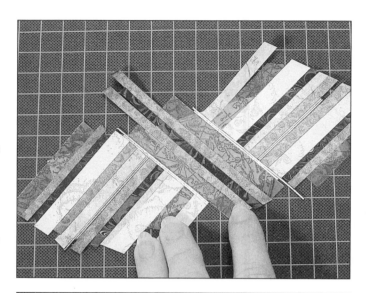

Love with Words

Use hues of cream, gold, and burgundy to show just how much you care. Better yet, create one for an engagement, wedding, or anniversary because these sentimental creations have "I love you" written all over them.

Get Started:

craft knife • cutting mat • cards: white, cream • straight edge • pencil • scraps of organza: iridescent cream, gold • spray adhesive • scraps of edging lace, white • silk flowers and leaves: white, red • fine florist's wire • iridescent tissue • tacky glue • white paper • spraypaint, gold • organza ribbon: pink, gold • large-eyed needle • acrylic paint, pink • paintbrush • cardboard • pen top • cotton wool • scraps of cards: pale pink, deep pink • gold wire

Gift Box Card

1 Cut a rectangle of white card 11" × 5½". Score and then fold the card in half in the same way as for the bouquet card.

2 Roughly cut a 5½" square of cream organza. Glue it onto the center of the front of the card using spray adhesive.

3 Make two boxes from thick paper or thin card. Trace the lines from the diagram below onto the card or paper, using a pencil and ruler, and then cut out the shape, before folding and gluing the sides in place (Figure 1).

4 When the glue is dry, spraypaint the box gold. Glue a length of lace across the middle of one of the boxes: This will be the lid.

5 Tie a small bow using pink organza ribbon, and then thread another length of ribbon through the knot at the back using a large-eyed needle.

6 Glue the ribbon around the box, so that it is in the center of the lace with the bow in the middle of the box.

7 Cut four 2¾" squares of iridescent tissue. Place them one at a time into the other box, so that they are at different angles to one another: This is the base.

8 Add a small amount of tacky glue between the layers to hold them in place.

9 Glue a spray of small, red silk flowers inside the base.

10 Arrange the base and lid onto the front of the card and glue in place with tacky glue: The base should be flat on the card, and one corner of the lid should be resting on the base.

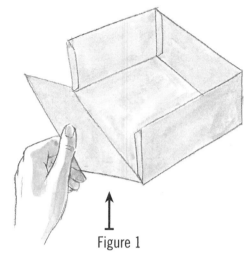

Figure 1

Bouquet Card

1 Using a craft knife and cutting mat, cut a rectangle of cream card 8¾" × 4⅜". Draw a fine pencil line halfway across the width of the card.

2 Score across this line using a straight edge and the back of the craft knife. The scored line should have just broken the top layer of the card, making it easier to fold in half.

3 Fold the card in half, lining up the edges of the card without putting pressure on the scored line. Check the alignment at the edges, then press the card along the score.

4 Roughly cut a 3½" square of gold organza. Glue this to the center of the front of the card with spray adhesive.

5 Glue a length of lace, vertically, down the center of the front of the card on top of the organza.

6 Bunch together a spray of small, white silk flowers and leaves. Bind the stems together by wrapping them with fine florist's wire.

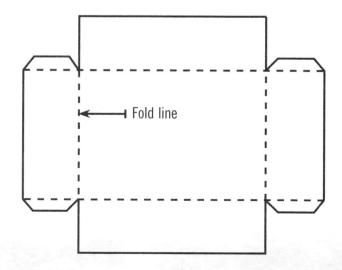

← → Fold line

7 Cut a 5½" square of iridescent tissue. Place the bouquet on the tissue, so that the flowers lie slightly diagonal across the center.

8 Wrap the sides of the tissue around the flowers, and bind tightly around the stems with fine wire.

9 Cut off the tissue 1" below the wire, then make a bow around the bouquet using pink ribbon.

10 Glue the bouquet diagonally onto the front of the card.

Heart Card

1 Cut a rectangle of cream card 7" × 6¼". Score and fold the card in half in the same way as you did for the gift box and bouquet cards.

2 Roughly cut a rectangle of gold organza 5¾" × 2⅜".

3 Glue it to the center on the front of the card using spray adhesive.

4 Using spray adhesive, glue a length of lace horizontally across the card's front, slightly below the middle of the card.

5 Paint a pen top using bright pink acrylic paint. Leave it to dry for the time the manufacturer of the paint recommends.

Remember: You may need several coats of paint to cover the original color.

6 Wrap gold organza ribbon two or three times around the pen top, gluing the ribbon ends to hold them in place. Fill the pen top with cotton wool.

7 Trace the large and small heart shapes below. Transfer the outlines to pale and deep pink card, and then cut them out.

8 Glue a length of gold wire onto the back of each heart.

9 Dab glue onto each of the heart's flower stems, and push them down into the cotton wool inside the painted pen top.

10 Glue the back of the pen top to the front of the card.

Dye Hard

Once you get the hang of creating dyed paper (see Dyed Paper technique on page 23), use your creation and experiment with this simple, elegant card.

Get Started:

chipboard (cardboard) • clear glue • dyed paper • rubber stamp • threads or fiber • doublestick tape • tall cardstock

Switch It Up

Add something different by trying colored wire strung with beads instead of using thread. The results will impress you!

1 Cut a 3" × 2" piece of chipboard and a smaller piece in the shape of a heart. Cover the pieces of board with a coat of clear glue.

2 Quickly apply the dyed paper to the board, allowing the paper to retain any creases or wrinkles. Repeat the steps on the heart-shaped piece.

3 Tear away the excess paper.

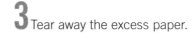

4 Stamp a few images on it.

5 Crisscross yarn or thread over the heart. Tie the thread together on the back side of the heart and secure with doublestick tape.

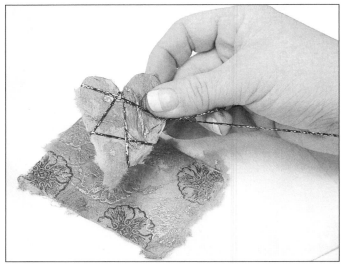

6 Apply a dab of glue to the board, then layer the heart on the board.

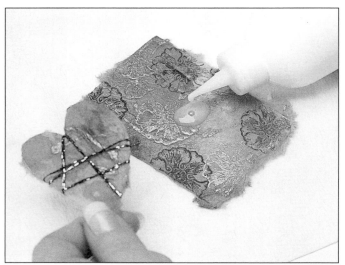

7 Add doublestick tape to the back of the square and apply to the cardstock.

Cut Out for You

You're allowed to cut corners on this one! With plenty of paper leftover for other card projects, put your ruler to work and send that special someone something straight from your heart.

Get Started:

rectangular stamp of your choice • cardstock • pigment ink • embossing powder • heat gun • craft knife • cutting mat • double-sided tape • notecard • tassel

1 Stamp an image in pigment ink on cardstock.

2 Sprinkle embossing powder over the still-wet ink and shake off any excess. Use a heat gun to melt the embossing powder.

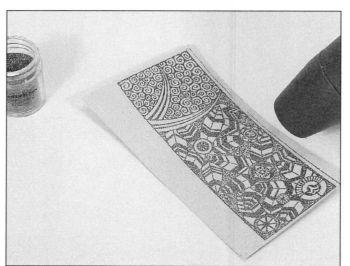

3 To start making a pattern, use a sharp craft knife to cut the image in half vertically.

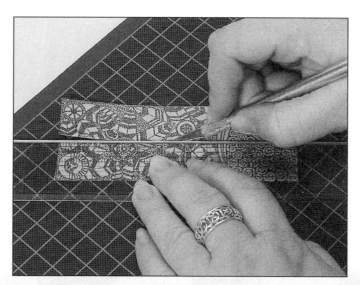

Switch It Up

To create a more intricate pattern, cut the pieces into smaller sections and use several colors of paper or embossing powders.

4 Cut the pieces in half again.

5 Reheat the edges of each piece to reseal the embossing. This will keep the embossing from flaking off along the edges.

6 Affix double-sided masking tape to the back of each stamped piece. Layer the pieces onto contrasting cardstock, leaving ¼" between the pieces.

7 Adhere the cardstock to a dark-colored notecard. Tie on a matching tassel.

Key to My Greeting

This card is perfect to give to someone you love, as the key represents the opening of words from your heart.

Get Started:

chipboard (cardboard) • assorted-color cardstock • fabric bond • iron • scissors • assorted fibers (threads, ribbons, yarn) • key • sculpture paper (see technique on page 21) • doublestick tape

1 Start this project by cutting a rectangle of cardstock or chipboard and a piece of bonding material 3" × 4". Place the bonding piece on the front of the cardstock. Iron the two pieces together. When cool, remove the backing from the bond.

Remember: Metallic threads add a special flair to natural fibers and silk ribbons.

2 Cut an array of beautifully colored threads, narrow silk ribbons, and fancy yarns to lay on top of the cardstock. Leave at least ⅛" overhang on all sides. Cover the piece generously. Add bonding pieces as needed over the fibers. Iron over the entire piece.

3 Tie on a piece of chenille or ribbon to an old key or charm.

4 Tie the key to the fiber piece. Wrap extra chenille around the base.

5 Take a piece of sculpture paper and fold the edges back to the desired size.

6 Add a light-colored layer of cardstock.

Remember: Try not to trim the fibers too evenly so as to retain the ragged appearance.

7 Trim away any excess fibers.

8 Add doublestick tape to the back of the fiber piece. Apply it to the card.

Part Five

Get Festive:
Cards for Holidays

Triangle Tumblers

This card is fun, quick, and easy to create. Send it out as your holiday card!

 Get Started:

small stamps of your choice • cardstock • assorted paper in various colors and patterns • dye ink • double-sided masking tape • 8½" × 11" Cosmic vellum • hole punch • tassel

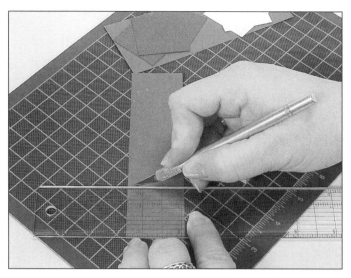

1 Begin with three different colors of paper. Cut at least three 1½" squares from each color. Cinnamon, forest, and white are the colors used here for this particular project.

2 Use one color of ink with different stamp patterns for all the squares. Allow the ink to dry.

3 Cut the squares diagonally to make triangles.

Continues

4 Apply small pieces of double-sided masking tape to the backs of the triangles. Place the triangles, in alternating colors, on a tall card.

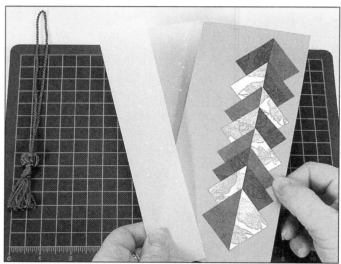

5 Make a vellum overlay. It goes over the card and tucks under the triangles. To do this, fold a piece of 8½" × 11" Cosmic vellum in half vertically and trim to fit the tall card. Unfold the vellum and lay your ruler along the fold so that the ruler is on the right of the fold. Cut away the vellum to the right of the ruler, leaving about 1½" excess. Fold the vellum overlay onto the card.

6 Attach the overlay with a tassel by punching two holes on the crease of the card and the overlay.

Glitter Christmas

Spice up the season and spread some joy with glittery trees, stars, and holly! Your friends and family will love these homemade treats, and you're bound to enjoy every second you spend creating them!

Get Started:

envelopes and card, brown • paper napkins, red and green • rolling pin • sponge • star-shaped stamp • writing paper, white • powder poster paints, red and green • tinsel, gold • metallic paint, gold • thin ribbon, gold • rubbing paste, gold • blank stencil card • light box or window • embossing tool • craft knife • cutting mat • pencil • ruler • newspaper • tacky glue • water

Figure 2

Figure 3

Figure 1

Figure 4

Remember: You will need to make five sheets of red paper and five sheets of green paper in order to make the Glitter Christmas Cards. To learn how to make paper, see page 14. To color the paper, tear red paper napkins into small squares and add them to the pulp and stir well. For stronger color, add red powdered poster paint to the paper pulp, and stir to mix in powder well. Do the same with the green paper. Remove some strands from the tinsel, and drop them on the surface of the pulp before making each sheet of paper.

Holly Card

1 Cut a piece of red handmade paper 7" × 10", giving the edges a torn look. To achieve this look, fold the paper where you want the tear to be and dampen with water. Then, tear along the fold and crease the paper exactly in half.

2 Using Figure 1, trace the holly design onto the stencil card and cut along the outlines, leaving the leaf and berry-shaped holes cut in the stencil card.

3 Tear a piece of green paper 3¼" × 5". Hold the stencil firmly on the middle of the paper. Using a small piece of sponge, dab gold rubbing paste onto the paper through the holes cut in the stencil. Leave the card to dry.

4 Place the paper with rubbing paste, with the stencil still in position, on a light box (or against a window) so that the stencil is face down. Work from the reverse side of the design.

5 Draw around the edges of the design, using an embossing tool, pressing as hard as you can without tearing the paper.

Remember: Depending on the thickness of the paper, it may not be possible to see through it. If this is the case, you should "feel" your way round the edges of the stencil with the tool.

6 Rub over the rest of the design as though coloring with a pencil, making the leaves and berries slightly concave.

7 Carefully remove the stencil from the green paper. Glue the embossed green paper onto the center of the front of the red card.

8 To finish the card, cut a piece of white writing paper slightly smaller than the card; fold it in half, and glue it inside the card along the spine.

Matching Envelope

1 To make the envelope that goes with the holly card, cut a piece of red paper 2½" × 2¾". Then, fold the paper where you want the tear to be, dampen with water, and tear along the fold. Fold the paper exactly in half.

2 Glue this piece of red paper to the top left-hand corner of the envelope.

3 Tear a piece of green paper 1¾" × 1¾". Using Figure 2, trace the small holly leaf.

4 Stencil and emboss the holly leaf onto the paper as you did with the holly design for the card.

5 Glue it to the center of the red paper on the envelope.

Matching Envelope

1 To make the matching envelope, tear a piece of red paper 2¼" × 2¼". Glue it at an angle on the top left-hand corner of the envelope so that it looks like a diamond.

2 Stencil and emboss the gold star from the top of the Christmas tree onto a piece of green handmade paper.

3 Cut the star out with a margin of ⅛" and glue it to the center of the red diamond.

Christmas Tree Card

1 Cut a piece of red handmade paper 7" × 10" by tearing the edges as you did with the holly card. Fold the paper in half.

2 Using Figure 3, trace the Christmas tree design.

3 Cut a piece of green paper slightly larger than the tree; stencil and emboss the tree onto the paper.

4 Cut around the embossed tree being sure to leave a margin of about ⅛" around the edges.

5 Glue the tree onto the card.

6 To finish, cut a piece of white writing paper slightly smaller than the card; fold it in half, and glue it inside the card along the spine.

Star Card

1 Cut a piece of green paper 7" × 10", tearing the edges as done with the holly and tree cards. Fold the paper in half.

2 Tear a piece of red paper 3" × 5½". Glue the paper to the front of the green card.

3 Stencil and emboss the star onto red paper, using Figure 4 to help you trace the shape.

4 Cut out the star leaving a small margin of red paper around the design.

5 Cut out the center of the star using a craft knife. Put the smaller star to one side.

6 Trace the size of the cut-out star onto green paper. Glue the green star to the center of the card. Set smaller star aside for envelope.

Matching Envelope

1 Tear a 2" × 2½" rectangle of green paper, and glue it to the top left corner of the envelope.

2 Tear a 1¼" × 1½" rectangle of red paper and glue this to the center of the green.

3 Glue the small star, cut from the larger, onto the envelope.

Gift Wrap

1 Paint a thin layer of gold paint onto the surface of your star-shaped stamp. Then press the stamp down firmly onto a piece of handmade paper.

2 Add more paint to the stamp. Repeat stamping until the paper is covered with stars.

3 Allow the paper to dry, untouched for about an hour. The paper can now be used as gift wrap!

Tags

1 Cut a rectangle from stamped paper and cut the same sized rectangle from the stencil card.

2 Glue the two together and punch a hole in one corner.

3 Thread with gold ribbon. Voilà! Tags!

Snowy Snowmen

Get into the holiday spirit and spread some cheer with this very creative card. Be sure that you don't use a picture from an ink jet printer—it won't work. Have fun!

Get Started:

snowflake stamp • color photocopy of a design of your choice • heavy clear self-adhesive laminate or acetate • bone folder • craft knife or scissors • bowl of water big enough to hold laminate • square notecard • metallic gel ink pen • double-sided clear tape • double-sided foam tape • copy of a small vintage photograph

1 Apply the photocopy to the sticky side of a piece of heavy clear laminate.

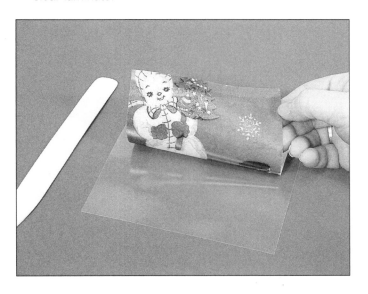

Switch It Up

Once you've tried this project, try collaging several images together directly on the sticky side of the laminate. Apply metallic pens, powdered pigments, or gold leaf foils to the sticky side of the acetate for a dramatic effect.

2 Carefully burnish the back side of the copy with a bone folder or brayer.

3 Trim any excess laminate.

4 Immerse the entire piece in tap water for at least three minutes.

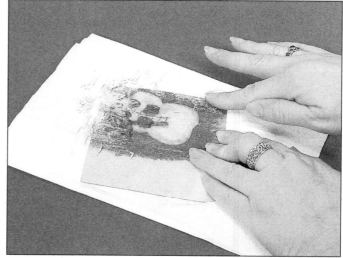

5 Place the piece (shiny side down) onto paper towels. Begin rubbing the paper off the laminate with the tips of your fingers. It is very important not to use a sharp object to do the rubbing because it could scrape the veneer. Be sure to remove as much paper as possible. If you see a felt-like residue when the piece is dry, dip the piece in water again and continue rubbing.

Remember: Keep your fingers wet when rubbing off the paper. This helps speed up the removal process. The finished veneer should be translucent when all the paper has been rubbed off. Notice that the portion that was white is now clear.

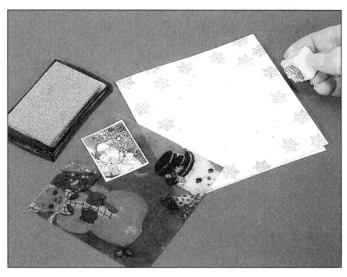

6 Stamp a border around a square card.

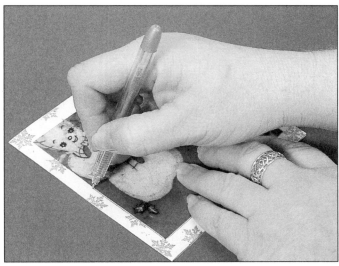

7 Use a metallic gel ink pen to trace a border on the note-card around the trimmed laminate.

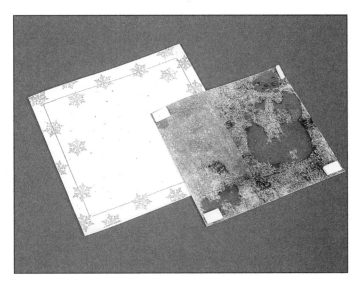

8 Finish the card by using clear double-sided tape to adhere the small photocopy of a vintage photograph to the veneer. To create a 3-D effect, use double-sided foam tape squares to adhere the veneer to the card. You can also use clear double-sided tape.

Leaves of Autumn

Tie this one to a special gift, or give it alone. The colors are representative of all things that remind us of fall.

 Get Started:

assorted leaf punches • large shipping tag • Krylon gold leafing pen • silk ribbon • tall cardstock • gold leaf • brown pigment ink • cold laminate • stiff brush • tissue • piece of paper • craft knife or scissors • doublestick tape or glue

Remember: Turning a punch upside down will make positioning the shapes much easier.

1 Find a large shipping tag. Remove the string. Punch out most of the surface of the tag with an array of leaf craft punches. (These punches are widely available from craft, stamp, and scrapbooking stores.)

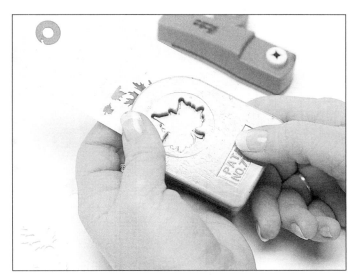

2 Once you finish punching, apply a piece of laminating sheet to the back of the tag. Trim away any excess laminate.

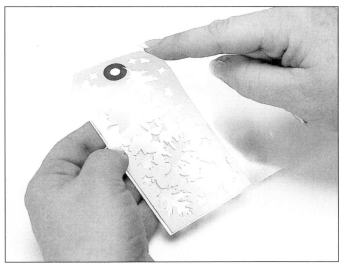

3 On the sticky side of the tag, lay gold leaf.

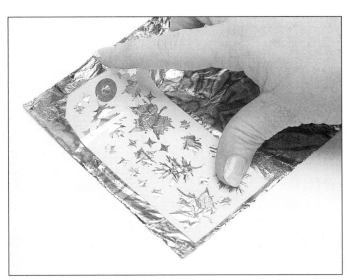

4 Press the gold leaf firmly into the crevices. Gently use a stiff brush to remove any excess foil.

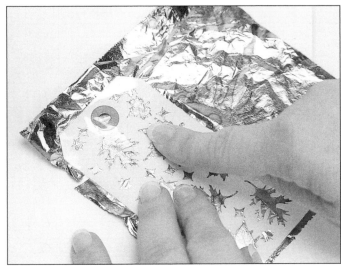

Continues

Remember: Pigment ink works well for this particular card since the paper on most tags is uncoated. Also, the ink wipes off the foil effortlessly.

5 Using a brown pigment ink pad, color the tag. It is suggested that you apply the ink after every image has been punched. That way it will cover the cut edges of each image.

6 Remove any excess ink from the gold leaf with a tissue.

7 Cover the brown reinforcement. Edge the tag with a gold leafing pen.

8 Lay the tag on a contrasting piece of paper. Trim to leave a ¼" edge.

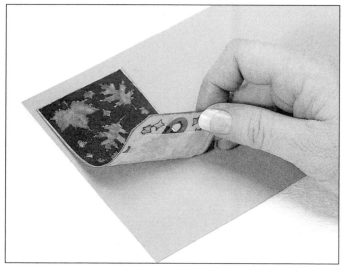

9 Add a coordinating ribbon and lay the tag element on a tall card.

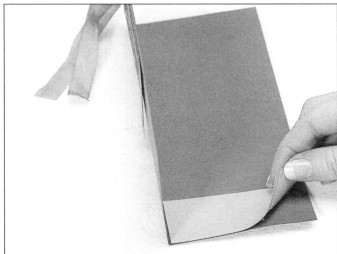

10 For more pizzazz, add a strip of the contrasting paper to the inside bottom of the card.

11 Finish the card by punching a few tiny leaves along the bottom front edge of the card.

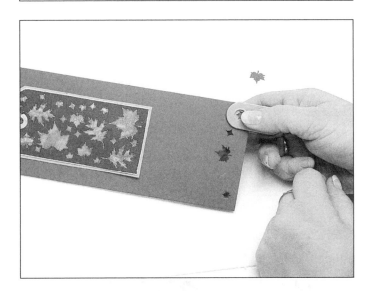

Switch It Up

Vivid colors and simple geo-metric punches work well on birthday cards.

Lovey Dovey Face

This card is perfect for Valentine's Day—or just because you want to say "I love you." Or, forget love—send it to someone who should know that you've been thinking of him or her . . .

 Get Started:

1 word stamp • 1 large face stamp • pigment ink pad • embossing powder • heat gun • water-soluble crayons • small paintbrush • bowl of water • double-sided masking tape

1 Stamp a background with a fun word stamp. Try using two light shades of dye inks. Don't use more than three colors. Limiting the colors will keep the pattern harmonious.

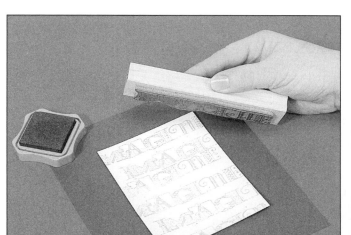

2 Using the large face stamp, stamp using a pigment ink.

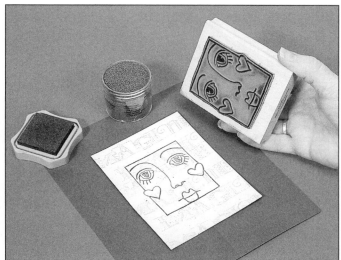

3 Cover the image in embossing powder. Shake off any excess.

4 Heat the powder thoroughly and allow the piece to cool.

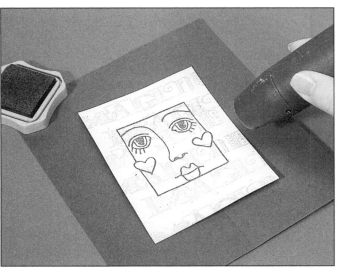

5 Color in the open sections of the stamps with colors similar to those used in the background.

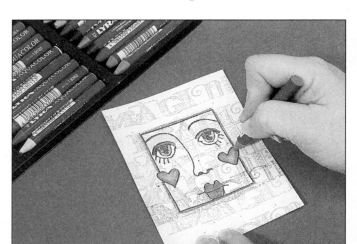

6 Blend the crayon colors using a slightly damp paintbrush.

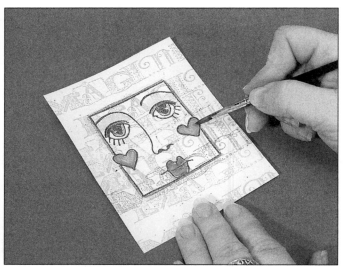

7 Add a rim of green around the outside edge of the face stamp. Blend it with some water.

8 When the piece has dried, trim off any excess from the edges. Apply the piece to a notecard with double-sided tape.

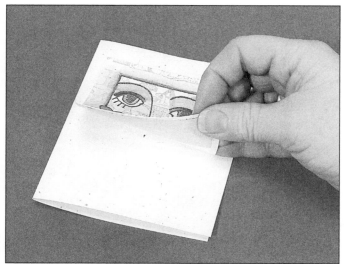

Glossary

acetate: from acetic acid; used in laminating

acrylic ink: used for decorating; this can be mixed together with Diamond Glaze and gesso as well as many other kinds of paint

awl: a tool used to make holes in fabric

beads: decorations used to enhance the card; used often in jewelry making and made in a variety of sizes and colors

binder: powdered pigments need this in order to adhere to materials; Diamond Glaze is an example of one

bone folder: a tool used to score and smooth paper

brayers: used to evenly spread ink, there are ones made of wood, acrylic, sponge, and hard rubber, and each yields a different result

bucket: used for soaking scrap paper to make paper pulp

burnish: polishing or smoothing whether by using a tool or one's hands

cardstock: a type of material used for cards

chipboard: board created from discarded paper

clean bricks or **heavy weights**: used on top of hardboard to apply pressure to the stack of paper

cold laminate: a heavy acetate that is sticky on one side

craft knife and **cutting mat**: used to cut a card neatly and accurately

double-sided tape: used for applying surface decoration or for gluing an insert in a card; types include mosaic tape, cellophane double-sided tape, and double-sided foam tape

dye re-inker: small bottles of ink used to refill dye-based inkpads

embellishments: decorations or enhancements for crafts

embossing powder: required in most rubberstamping projects; use with a heat gun to add dimension to cards

eyelets: like grommets, but a single unit

fabric bond: used to adhere fibrous materials together

gesso: primer paint, used for a primer with canvas and Styrofoam

glue gun: used for attaching heavier objects like jewels, tiles, and beads to the front of a card, envelope, or tag

hardboard: used to sandwich the newly made paper

heat gun: used to aid in adhering materials

ink: pigmented liquid used for printing; types include dye-based, solvent-based, and pigment

kitchen cloths: used between each sheet of paper to soak up the water and make it easier to move while wet

Kraft cardstock: a type of cardstock

Krylon: a type of paint pen

length of wood or **hand liquidizer**: used for beating paper pulp to a smooth, creamy paste

mica tiles: compressed layers of mica for decoration or for protection over photos, meant to be cut and layered

mold and deckle: two identical wooden frames, one covered with net, which fit exactly together and are used to collect paper pulp from the vat

newspaper: used to protect the work surface

paint pens: used for embellishing; applied in pen form and sometimes brushed; Krylon is a type of paint pen

paper: materials like wood, rags, and grasses processed to form flexible sheets

pastels and **water-soluble crayons**: used to decorate cards and add color

PearlEx: a type of powdered pigment

picture pebble: similar to a glass marble, it has only one flat surface; when placed over an image, it magnifies the design

plastic sheet: used to cover the work surface

powdered pigment: PearlEx is an example of this

punches and cutters: used to add embellishment; made to punch or cut in a variety of shapes and designs

rolling pin: used to give wet sheets of paper a smooth finish

ROXS: used to add dimension to cards

rubber stamp: raised characters or designs imprinted in rubber, usually attached to a wooden handle used for decoration and embellishment

score and fold: to mark the surface with parallel cuts and bend

shrink plastic: used with heat to coat, protect, and enhance a card

Styrofoam: a type of foam

tacky glue: used for applying surface decoration or for gluing an insert in a card

tassels and **cords**: used for embellishment and decoration for cards

templates: made from brass or plastic as a guide to create cards, envelopes, or tags

vat: a plastic tray larger than the mold and deckle that will hold sufficient paper pulp to make a sheet of paper

vellum: a heavy, off-white parchment material made from calfskin, lambskin, or kidskin

watch crystals: used to hold other items like beads and available in plastic; a great embellishment for cards

Resources

Stamp, Paper, and Ink Companies

The following is a listing of Web sites and business addresses where you can find the supplies needed to create greeting cards. Be aware that some of these businesses, those that sell rubber stamps especially, have different policies concerning copyrights, catalogs, stamps, and supplies. Be sure to inquire about these policies in person, via telephone, or on the Web.

Acey Duecy
P.O. Box 194
Ancram, NY 12502

Alice in Rubberland
P.O. Box 9262
Seattle, WA 98109

American Art Stamp
3892 Del Amo Blvd.
Suite 701
Torrance, CA 90503
(310) 371-6593
www.americanartstamp.com

Art Gone Wild
3110 Payne Ave.
Cleveland, OH 44114
(800) 945-3950

Carmen's Veranda/Postscript
P.O. Box 1539
Placentia, CA 92871
www.carmensveranda.com

Claudia Rose
15 Baumgarten Rd.
Saugerties, NY 12477
(914) 679-9235

Coffee Break Designs
P.O. Box 34281
Indianapolis, IN 46234

**ColorBox / Clearsnap
/ Ancient Page**
P.O. Box 98
Anacortes, WA 98221
(360) 293-6634
www.clearsnap.com

**Craft Connection / Great
American Stamp Store**
1015 Post Road E.
Westport, CT 06880
(203) 221-1229

Craft World
No. 8 North St., Guildford
Surrey GU1 4AF
England
Tel: 07000 757070

**The Creative Block /
Stamper's Anonymous**
20613 Center Ridge Rd.
Rocky River, OH 44116
(440) 333-7941

Curtis Uyeda/Curtis' Collection
3326 St. Michael Dr.
Palo Alto, CA 94306

Denami Design
P.O. Box 5617
Kent, WA 98064
(253) 639-2546

Draggin' Ink
P.O. Box 24135
Santa Barbara, CA 93121
(805) 966-5297

February Paper
P.O. Box 4297
Olympia, WA 98501
(360) 330-6831

Great American Stamp Store
1015 Post Road E.
Westport, CT 06880
(203) 221-1229

Gumball Graphics
1417 Creighton Ave.
Dayton, OH 45420
(513) 258-2663

Hobby Crafts
River Court, Southern Sector
Bournemouth Int'l. Airport
Christ Church
Dorset BH23 6SE
England
Tel: 0800 272387

Hot Potatoes
2805 Columbine Place
Nashville, TN 37204
(615) 269-8002
www.hotpotatoes.com

Jacquard Products
Rupert, Gibbon and Spiders, Inc.
P.O. Box 425
Healdsburg, CA 95448
(800) 442-0455
www.jacquardproducts.com
(You can find PearlEx here.)

JudiKins
17803 S. Harvard Blvd.
Gardena, CA 90248
(310) 515-1115
www.judikins.com
(You can find Diamond Glaze here.)

Krylon Products
101 Prospect Ave., NW
Cleveland, OH 44115
(800) 797-3332

Lighthouse Memories
(909) 879-0218
www.lighthousememories.com

Love You to Bits/Tin Can Mail
P.O. Box 5748
Redwood City, CA 90248
(800) 546-LYTB

Magenta
351 Blain
Mont-Saint Hilaire
Quebec, Canada J3H3B4
(514) 446-5253
www.magentarubberstamps.com

McGill
(800) 982-9884
www.mcgillinc.com

Marvy-Uchida
3535 Del Amo Blvd.
Torrance, CA 90503
(800) 541-5877
www.uchida.com

Meer Image
P.O. Box 12
Arcata, CA 95518
www.meerimage.com

Moe Wubba
P.O. Box 1445
Dept. B
San Luis Obispo, CA 93406
(805) 547-1MOE

On the Surface
P.O. Box 8026
Wilmette, IL 60091

Pam Bakke Paste Papers
303 Highland Drive
Bellingham, WA 98225
(360) 738-4830

Paper Parachute
P.O. Box 91385
Portland, OR 97291-0385

paula best Rubberstamps
445 La Coches Court
Morgan Hill, CA 95037
(408) 778-1018
www.paulabest.com

Postmodern Design
P.O. Box 720416
Norman, OK 73070

**Postscript Studio /
Carmen's Veranda**
P.O. Box 1539
Placentia, CA 92871
(888) 227-6367
www.postscriptstudio.com

Rubber Baby Buggy Bumpers
1331 W. Mountain Ave.
Fort Collins, CO 80521
(970) 224-3499

Rubber Monger
P.O. Box 1777
Snowflake, AZ 85937

Rubbermoon
P.O. Box 3258
Hayden Lake, ID 83835
(208) 772-9772
www.rubbermoon.com

Rubber Zone
P.O. Box 10254
Marina del Ray, CA 90295
www.rubberzone.com

Ruby Red Rubber
P.O. Box 2076
Yorba Linda, CA 92885
(714) 970-7584

Scattered Pictures
(503) 252-1888

Skycraft Designs / Papers
26395 S. Morgan Rd.
Estacada, OR 97023
(503) 630-7173

Speedball
P.O. Box 5157
2226 Speedball Rd.
Statesville, NC 28687
(704) 838-1475
www.speedballart.com

Stampacadabra
5091 N. Fresno St.
Suite 133
Fresno, CA 93710
(209)227-7247

Stamp Addicts
Park Lane Lodge, Park Lane
Gamlingay
Bedfordshire SG19 3PD
England
Phone/fax: 01767 650329
www.stampaddicts.com

Stampa Rosa Inc.
2322 Midway Dr.
Santa Rosa, CA 95405
(707) 527-8267
www.stamparosa.com

Stamp Camp
P.O. Box 222091
Dallas, TX 75222
(214) 830-0020

A Stamp in the Hand
20630 S. Leapwood Ave.
Suite B
Carson, CA 90746
(310) 329-8555
www.astampinthehand.com

Stamp Your Art Out
9685 Kenwood Rd.
Cincinnati, OH 45242
www.stampawayusa.com

Stamp Your Heart Out
141-C Harvard
Claremont, CA
(909) 621-4363
www.stampyourheart.com

Stampscapes
7451 Warner Ave.
#E124
Huntington Beach, CA 92647

Stamps Happen, Inc.
369 S. Acacia Ave.
Fullerton, CA 92631
(714) 879-9894

The Studio
P.O. Box 5681
Bellevue, WA 98006

Toybox Rubber Stamps
P.O. Box 1487
Healdsburg, CA 95448
(707) 431-1400

Twenty Two
6167 N. Broadway
#322
Chicago, IL 60660

USArtquest
7800 Ann Arbor Rd.
Grass Lake, MI 49240
(517) 522-6225
www.usartquest.com

Viva Las Vegastamps
1008 East Sahara Ave.
Las Vegas, NV 89104
(702) 836-9118
www.stampo.com

Wilde Ideas
(800) 558-8680
www.wilde-ideas.com

Worth Repeating
227 N. East St.
New Auburn, WI 54757
(715) 237-2011

Zettiology / The Studio Zine
P.O. Box 5681
Bellevue, WA 98006
www.zettiology.com

Books

30-Minute Rubber Stamp Workshop by Sandra McCall
Creative Rubber Stamping Techniques by MaryJo McGraw
Creative Stamping with Mixed Media Techniques by
    Sherrill Kahn
Greeting Cards for Every Occasion by MaryJo McGraw
Making Cards with Rubber Stamps by Maggie Wright
Making Gifts with Rubber Stamps by Sandra McCall
*Making Greeting Cards with Rubber
    Stamps* by MaryJo McGraw
Rubber Stamp Extravaganza by Vesta Abel
Rubber Stamp Gifts by Judy Claxton
Rubber Stamped Jewelry by Sharilyn Miller
Stamp Your Stuff! by MaryJo McGraw
Storytelling with Rubber Stamps by Joanna Campbell-Slan

Publications

The Rubberstamper
225 Gordons Corner
Rd. P.O. Box 420
Manalapan, NJ
07726-0420
(800) 969-7176
www.therubberstamper.com

Rubberstampmadness
408 SW Monroe #210
Corvallis, OR 97330
(541) 752-0075
www.rsmadness.com

***Rubberstamp Source-
book & Travelers Guide
to Rubberstamping***
Cornucopia Press
4739 University Way NE
Suite 1610-A
Seattle, WA 98105
(206) 528-8120

***Stamper's Sampler &
Somerset Studio***
22992 Millcreek, Suite B
Laguna Hills, CA
(714) 380-7318
www.somersetstudio.com

Vamp Stamp News
P.O. Box 386
Hanover, MD 21076-0386
vampstamp@prodigy.net

Acknowledgments

A very special thanks to all of the contributors in this publication, specifically:

MaryJo McGraw for the following projects:

Corset Creation, page 28
Mini Message, page 32
Beatnik Terrific, page 43
Bead Intrigue, page 48
Post Your Hello, page 55
Wonder Women, page 62
Trippin' Triptych, page 64
Crystal Memory, page 70
Mica Heirloom, page 75
Picture Pebble, page 80
Framed Gals, page 90
Chinese Charm, page 94
Doggy Diorama, page 98
Circle of Fun, page 101
Time Flies, page 105
Pieces of Me, page 110
Dye Hard, page 116
Cut Out for You, page 119
Key to My Greeting, page 122
Triangle Tumblers, page 126
Snowy Snowmen, page 134
Leaves of Autumn, page 138
Lovey Dovey Face, page 142

Jill Millis for the following projects:

Flora and Fauna Fun, page 36
Glitter Christmas, page 129

Cheryl Owen for the following projects:

Planting Greetings, page 51
Flower Power, page 86
Love with Words, page 113

Jan Cox and **John Underwood** for the following project:

Celestial Creations, page 58

Index

the best in
creative greeting cards
from *North Light Books!*

GREETING CARDS
for **EVERY OCCASION**
MaryJo McGraw

23 FUN AND EASY **Rubber Stamp** PROJECTS

Create personalized greeting cards!

Renowned crafter MaryJo McGraw shares her most creative card ideas. With complete, step-by-step instructions and 23 detailed projects, you'll find it easy to make your sentiments more personal and meaningful.

#32580-K • $24.99

Be sure to look for these creative greeting card titles:

Vintage Greeting Cards with MaryJo McGraw
#32583-K • $23.99

Creative Correspondence
#32277-K • $19.99

Making Cards in a Weekend
#31665-K • $14.99

The Big Book of Handmade Cards and Gift Wrap
#33215-K • $21.99

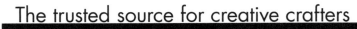

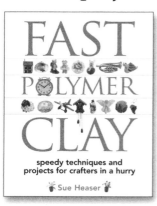
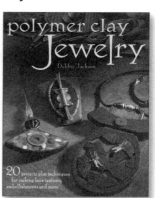
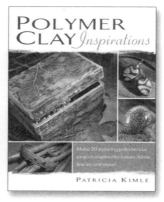

the best in

wedding crafts & inspirations
from *North Light Books,* *Memory Makers Books* and *Betterway Books!*

Make your wedding a unique and memorable event!

You'll discover over 50 personalized projects to make your wedding one-of-a-kind. Easy-to-follow instructions guide you in creating professional-looking invitations and coordinated projects such as guest books, party favors, decorations, keepsakes and more. From whimsical and contemporary to elegant and sophisticated, you're sure to find inspiration to reflect your personal style for a wedding that is truly your own.

#70603-K • $19.99

Wedding PAPERCRAFTS
Create Your Own Invitations, Decorations and Favors to Personalize Your Wedding
From the Editors of North Light Books

Be sure to look for these wedding craft titles:

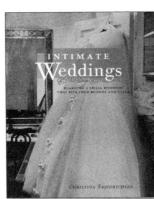

Intimate Weddings
#70642-K • $14.99

Scrapbooking Your Wedding
#33211-K • $22.99

New Inspirations in Wedding Florals
#70582-K • $19.99

How to Have a Big Wedding on a Small Budget
#70594-K • $14.99

The trusted source for brides-to-be

Savings Code TK04EWCB

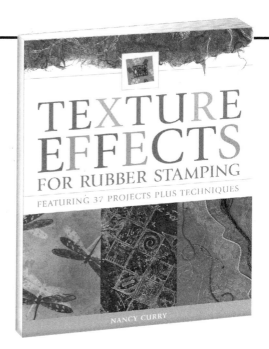

the best in

rubber stamping techniques
from *North Light Books!*

It's easy to add rich beauty to personalized cards and gifts!

Add elegant, rich textures to your handmade greeting cards and gifts. With complete, step-by-step instructions and 37 stylish projects, you'll find a wonderful mix of new texture approaches, dimensional effects and decorative accents to make your personalized cards and gifts more memorable.

#33014-K • $22.99

Be sure to look for these rubber stamping titles:

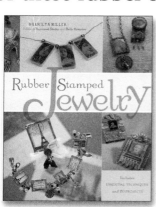

Creative Stamping with Mixed Media Techniques
#32315-K • $22.99

Rubber Stamped Jewelry
#32415-K • $22.99

Stamp Your Stuff!
#32432-K • $12.99

30-Minute Rubber Stamp Workshop
#32142-K • $24.99

.Savings Code
TL04ERSB